LANCASTER COUNTY

TEXT BY ED KLIMUSKA

PHOTOGRAPHY BY KEITH BAUM AND JERRY IRWIN

FOREWORDS BY PATRICK F. NOONAN AND DONALD B. KRAYBILL

VOYAGEUR PRESS

A Pictorial Discovery Guide

DEDICATION

To my parents
For all their help
—Ed Klimuska

To the love of my life Carol and my precious children David and Katie,
whose support and sacrifice have carried me through this project.
—Keith Baum

This edition published in 1998 by Voyageur Press, an imprint of MBI Publishing Company,
Galtier Plaza, Suite 200, 380 Jackson Street, St. Paul, MN 55101-3885 USA

MBI Publishing Company titles are also available at discounts in bulk quantity for industrial or sales-promotional use.
For details write to Special Sales Manager at MBI Publishing Company, Galtier Plaza, Suite 200, 380 Jackson Street,
St. Paul, MN 55101-3885 USA

Edited by Todd R. Berger
Designed by Kristy Tucker
Printed in Hong Kong

Library of Congress Cataloging-in-Publication Data

Klimuska, Ed, 1946–
Lancaster County / text by Ed Klimuska ; photography by Keith Baum and Jerry Irwin.
Includes bibliographical references and index
ISBN-13: 978-0-89658-397-9 (pbk.)
ISBN-10: 0-89658-392-9 (Hardcover) — ISBN-10: 0-89658-397-X (pbk.)
1. Lancaster County (Pa.) —Civilization. 2.) Lancaster County (Pa.)—Social life and customs.
3. Lancaster County (Pa.)—Pictorial works.
I. Baum, Keith, 1961– . II. Irwin, Jerry. III. Title.
F157.L2K64 1998 98-14320
974.8'15—dc21 CIP

Front cover photo: © Keith Baum.
Back cover photos, counter-clockwise from upper left: Photo © Jerry Irwin; Photo © Keith Baum; Photo © Keith Baum; Photo © Keith Baum; Photo © Jerry Irwin

Page 1: The Main Street of Lititz in northern Lancaster County exudes historic Americana charm. (Photo © Keith Baum)

TABLE OF CONTENTS

Acknowledgments

I am indebted to many Lancaster County people for reviewing chapters, supplying information, and sharing their ideas to shape this book project. Particular thanks go to Ronald Bailey, Darvin Boyd, Lucinda Hampton, Clyde McMillan-Gamber, Glen Mohler, Alan Musselman, Donald Robinson, Stephen Scott, Willis Shirk, Bruce Shoemaker, Charlotte "Chotty" Sprenkle, Scott Standish, and Carolyn Wenger and her staff at the Lancaster Mennonite Historical Society.

Two other individuals, Tom Daniels and Amos Hoover, provided special help. Daniels is the director of the Lancaster County Agricultural Preserve Board and an effective spokesman for farmland preservation not only in his community but throughout the country. A retired farmer, Hoover is the thoughtful keeper of the private Muddy Creek Farm Library and an authority on Old Order Mennonite culture who gives generously of his time.

Also, my deepest thanks go to Keith Baum and Jerry Irwin. They are talented photographers and tireless workers. Their exceptional images have captured the people, places, and passions of Lancaster County better than any writer could have hoped for.

—Ed Klimuska

I thank God for the privilege of growing up in and photographing a special place like Lancaster County. It is my hope that this book can play a small part in preserving the county's beauty and diversity for generations to come.

I owe a debt of gratitude to Todd Berger, Michael Dregni, and all of those at Voyageur Press who worked so hard to give us this wonderful opportunity. My deepest thanks to those who have assisted me personally and professionally: Marty Heisey, Rick Hertzler, Jack Leonard, and the crew at Lancaster Newspapers; Mark Mentzer at Perfect Image; and the dedicated staffs at Coe Camera, Delta Color, Filmet, and Hirtech. I am grateful for the love and encouragement of the Baum, Thomas, Nicholas, and my church families; for the patience of Dave and Liz Givens; and for the assistance of Dave Tucker, knight-errant extraordinaire.

I would never have pursued my love of photography without the influence of three special teachers, Dr. Ed Trayes of Temple University who taught me to "see," Steve Hofmann of Filmet who taught me to print, and Hank Deimer of Pequea Valley who let an ambitious high school student turn his physics closet into a darkroom.

Thanks to Allan Erselius, Nancy Smith, Nancy Stewart, and Cindy Hampton for putting the icing on the cake by allowing me to produce the Visitor's Bureau slide presentation based on this book. And finally, thanks to Ed and Jerry for your knowledge, insight, talent, and hard work. Together we made a book that makes me very proud to be a native of Lancaster County.

—Keith Baum

An Amish boy stands on a wagon loaded with pumpkins at the Leola Produce Auction. (Photo © Jerry Irwin)

FOREWORD

by Patrick F. Noonan

HEX SIGNS ON neat barns. Black buggies on Sunday mornings. Bright quilts ringed by primly capped women. These are the icons of Lancaster County. At the heart of the famous Pennsylvania Dutch country, Lancaster County attracts tens of thousands of tourists from throughout America and the rest of the world each year. The visitors, whose spending provides a major economic value to the county and the state, stay in towns and cities with colorful names—Bird-in-Hand, Paradise, Beartown.

Ever since my undergraduate days at Gettysburg College, I've been a visitor to Lancaster County. Today, my wife and I still enjoy Saturday shopping at the public market in Lancaster. During the summer months, we can stop at one of the county's many farm stands to take home corn, tomatoes, and just-picked berries, after a stay visiting auctions, prowling through antique shops, and traveling along country roads.

Yet for all the charm and special character of the county and region, it was the fertile land that first drew settlers to Lancaster County, and it is that same land, with its working farms, that draws visitors today. But now the county's beguiling rural landscape, with its gently rolling green fields and almost sparkling, family farms, is attracting a new wave of settlers that have made Lancaster the fastest growing county in Pennsylvania. Unlike the generations of farmers whose thoughtful, caring stewardship nurtured the land, the new residents form a phalanx of burgeoning growth that has the potential to overwhelm the county's

nationally renowned rural quality of life.

Lancaster County faces the dilemma of so many of America's communities: how to balance a traditional lifestyle with economic growth. In this compelling and informative look at the fabric of Lancaster County, author Ed Klimuska helps us realize just how much is at stake. Richly evocative photos by Keith Baum and Jerry Irwin let us see what life in Lancaster County means to its residents. Through the pages of *Lancaster County*, we learn about Old Order values and how they have shaped the lives of today's families. We visit roadside stands and farm markets where through most of the year locals and visitors alike enjoy a diverse bounty that ranges from asparagus to cheese, from shoofly pies to bright yellow mums. We journey through a countryside of cornfields and dairy farms where a land ethic of stewardship is rooted in family values.

Lancaster County's treasures are much more than historic buildings, horse-drawn buggies, and hand-twisted pretzels. Bald eagles nest along the Susquehanna River; on their long journey north, tundra swans by the thousands rest and feed in the county's freshwater wetlands. Woodlands, streams, and wildflower glens all add to the natural wonders of Lancaster County. And like the quiet, farming countryside, they, too, define the character of the county. This outdoor heritage also beckons visitors who enjoy the outdoors and whose economic impact is a positive addition to Lancaster County.

Above: *A toddler catches a few winks at the New Holland Fair. The youngsters are taking part in the baby parade. (Photo © Jerry Irwin)*

The writer and photographers take us to the farms that since the 1700s have been the foundation of the county and the source of its prosperity. It is the rich farmland, and the fact that Lancaster County is the most productive non-irrigated county in the nation, that has determined the character of this place. And, it is the generations of farm families with their strong values and passion for hard work, honesty, and community, that identify its residents.

As we approach the twenty-first century, the challenge of Lancaster County—to blend growth with tradition, to protect the fertile land that is the foundation of the county and its communities—is a challenge for all of us and, personally, for each of us. We are stewards of our land for our generation. It is our obligation as stewards to protect what we inherited for our children and their children. Across this great land we call America, communities are faced with similar hard choices. Can Lancaster County show us the way?

If history is any indicator, Lancaster County residents have always found a way. Almost three hundred years ago, Lancaster County's artisans built the first Conestoga wagons. These artfully designed wagons, named for the river that runs through the county, carried the people and goods of our emerging nation onto the frontiers. The wagons were a vital element in the growth of America. They were strong, intelligently crafted, and reflected the traditions of the people who made them. Today, as we begin a new millennium, Americans in Lancaster County and throughout the nation, are traveling toward a different frontier. The destination is not a new place, but rather a new idea: managing growth to enhance the quality of life. Just as the county's Conestoga wagons changed the face of America, so can the decisions the county's residents make today about their future serve as a model for communities from coast to coast.

So much is at risk, and the pressure for unplanned development and sprawl is great. Yet, Lancaster County's traditional values, strong agricultural economy, history of caring for the land, and its people can tip the scales in favor of appropriate, planned growth. I believe that Lancaster County will choose the path that protects its rich heritage and, in doing so, will create an unparalleled legacy for future generations.

Patrick F. Noonan is a trustee of the National Geographic Society and chairman of The Conservation Fund, one of the nation's leading land and water conservation organizations. He also serves as current chairman of the National Council of the American Farmland Trust.

FOREWORD

by Donald B. Kraybill

I AM A child of Lancaster County. Born and bred here, I have come to love this enchanting place, this "Garden Spot of the World." The spirit of this place has nurtured my character and shaped my values. And so it is a special honor and delight to write a foreword for this lovely book.

My childhood memories were shaped by the warm devotion of a Mennonite family. Early in the morning and again in the evening our family gathered in the stable to tend and milk our Guernsey cows. We tilled a hundred acres of rich limestone soil and on many August evenings shipped 1,000 baskets of freshly picked tomatoes off to a Campbell factory for soup and juice. Throughout hot summer months we stacked a thousand bales of hay in the sultry mows of our barn.

For spending money we picked worms—a penny apiece—from tobacco plants and trapped muskrats from nearby streams. We played bag tag in the barn, hunted cottontail rabbits, and skated on nearby ponds for recreational delight. Homemade root beer, shoofly pie, and scrapple added spice to our daily diet. Hot, dirty, and relentless, the farmwork was never done. Nevertheless, it was a good and satisfying life. Faith and family, work and community carved enduring values into the core of our character.

Intrigued by the call of a bigger world, I abandoned a seven-generation legacy of cows and plows to study sociology. I hoped to solve the mysteries of human behavior and better understand social systems. Bored by books, I often returned in the springtime to plow the fields and enjoy the scent of newly turned soil. Later, I came home to teach in the county and research its cultures and peoples. The farm still tugs and beckons, especially in April when seagulls search for grubs in the furrows of freshly tilled soil. Indeed, some say it is the soil—the precious limestone soil—that has shaped the character of this place.

Recent events have changed the character of Lancaster County. Developers and preservationists have struggled for the soul of Lancaster—the future of this place that recently appeared on the worldwide list of one hundred most endangered sites. Endangered or not, Lancaster is indeed a special place to all of us who call it home. But every place, of course, is special to the people that inhabit it. What distinguishes the character of this county?

Lancaster has been uniquely blessed by the hand of providence with an unusual mixture of people who have woven a delightful, cultural fabric. This rare confluence of people, places, and passions has bestowed a distinctive character on the Garden Spot.

A remarkable diversity of peoples and values intersect on this site:

Gigantic Wal-Mart stores sit amidst hundreds of roadside markets.
Multinational corporations coexist with thousands of Amish enterprises.
Lush fields of corn, soybeans, and alfalfa frame upscale suburban homes.

Above: Morning fog blankets the scenic eastern Lancaster County countryside. (Photo © Jerry Irwin)

Millions of tourists interact with native sons and daughters.

Superhighways slice through quaint villages and wildlife preserves.

High-performance cars and 18-wheelers traverse roads alongside horse-drawn buggies.

Hispanics and Asians reside alongside Old Order Mennonites.

Newcomers of many colors comingle with old German stock.

Institutions of higher education shadow dozens of one-room schools.

Old-fashioned barn raisings compete with national insurance companies.

Posh retirement communities border Amish homes that care for their elderly in homespun ways.

Daily prayers of devotion ascend amidst post-modern cynicism.

A strong sense of history persists in the face of rapid social change.

This intersection of diversity has carved a distinctive character into this place—a character forged by the virtues of hard work, extended family, community ritual, and religious devotion.

Beneath the public facade of the tourist booklets are pockets of hidden people—cultural islands—that rarely interact: Buddhists, Reformed Mennonites, Jews, Unitarians, African Americans, Bai-Hai, Chinese Americans, Methodists, and many more. The dozens of distinctive groups that call Lancaster home add to its plural character and bless it with cultural spice.

You will find some idyllic images in the pages that follow, but Lancaster is not heaven. We have our own share of drugs, homicides, and prisons. Reports of child abuse, domestic violence, and fraud also fill the pages of our papers. Hardly the vestibule of heaven, it is, nevertheless, an unusual place that has enjoyed a special measure of harmony, stability, and productivity. This exquisite book was produced by an extraordinary team of gifted artists. Award-winning photographers Jerry Irwin and Keith Baum have been capturing the people and places of Lancaster County for many years. Here they combine their talents to bring us stunning images of the cultural enclaves and natural beauty of the Garden Spot. Their breathtaking photos offer a grand and glorious tour of this remarkable county.

Veteran journalist, Ed Klimuska, interprets our journey with a lively text that flows from the lips and lives of local people. Seasoned by years of exposure to the life and lore of Lancaster's people, Klimuska crafts the story with deft skill and a creative eye. His winsome text provides both historical depth and cultural breadth.

This exceptional team leads us to unexpected vistas and out-of-the-way places as they seek to capture the character of this place. And capture it they do as they invite us to enjoy its beauty, meet its people, and sample its food. They lead us to quiltings, auctions, antiques, community festivals, bygone traditions, and local churches. In a variety of ways, they remind us that Lancaster's distinctive character is bound together by the strong threads of tradition, community, faith, and family.

This is a splendid book—an uncommon introduction to the people, places, and passions of Lancaster County. If you only buy one book on Lancaster County, this is the one to buy. Indeed, it stands in a class by itself. Visitors will value it as a reliable guide, and natives will discover new artifacts in the closet of their cultural home. To one and all, near and far, welcome to Lancaster County!

A native of Lancaster County, Donald B. Kraybill received his Ph.D. in sociology from Temple University. For many years he taught at Elizabethtown College where he also directed the Young Center for Anabaptist and Pietist Studies. He currently serves as Provost of Messiah College and is the author or editor of more than a dozen books including many on Amish and Mennonite culture.

LANCASTER COUNTY:
ITS PEOPLE, PLACES, AND PASSIONS

A SMALL TOWN welcomes the Fourth of July with one of the oldest celebrations in the nation, featuring thousands of flickering candles intensified by their twinkling reflection in the water below.

Beautiful handmade quilts go up for sale at a country auction.

A farmer harvests a lush field of corn on a golden October day.

Amish children carry lunchboxes and walk along country roads to their one-room schoolhouse where they learn the lessons of Old Order life.

A wildflower sanctuary showcases the biblical lilies of the field.

People crowd a stand at a farmers' market to buy garden-fresh vegetables.

Fire company volunteers sponsor an all-you-can-eat dinner featuring chicken and waffles, and people are prepared to wait an hour to get served because the homemade meal is so good and so plenty.

Main photo: *As the sun sets in southern Lancaster County, an Amish buggy moves along a country road. The Old Order horse-and-buggy is one of the symbols of Lancaster County. (Photo © Jerry Irwin)*
Inset: *This farm wagon roadside stand is loaded with pumpkins. Such family-operated farmer's stands are common in Lancaster County. This one operates on the honor system. (Photo © Keith Baum)*

A PAINTER IN FABRIC

Donna Albert is a textile artist whose award-winning quilts are sought after for their innovative design, visual impact, social statement, and artistic expression.

A painter in fabric, she creates vibrant artistic quilts.

Albert was raised in the village of Reinholds where her grandmother taught her to sew. Now, she lives in the town of Paradise where her quilts are examples of textile paradise.

In her creative world, fabric is never quite what it seems. Images, texture, and color leap from the surface of her quilts to make each one more than the sum of its parts.

One of her quilts, called "Who Can Doubt There Is a God?" depicts America's flower gardens and was chosen by the Museum of American Folk Art in New York City to be part of its permanent collection. Some

of her quilts, like the image-loaded "Pennsylvania Heartland," are inspired by her Lancaster County homeland. Her Red Diamond series explores the relationship between Amish quilts and modern painting.

In her words: "My Pennsylvania German heritage, which is deeply rooted in Lancaster County, has influenced my passion for color and simplicity of style, the need to create with my hands and a love of nature. My heritage inspires the images, the colors, and the textures of my work, translating into a personal fabric vocabulary."

Above: *Textile artist Donna Albert is an award-winning fabric designer. Her quilts appear in national museums and shows across the country. (Photo © Jerry Irwin)*

Lancaster County is blessed with a goodly heritage and exceptional diversity.

Donna Albert is a textile artist who understands her home county. She has designed a striking quilt, entitled "Pennsylvania's Heartland," that captures Lancaster County's heritage and diversity in an almost perfect snapshot. Her patchwork quilt has thirty images—farms, small towns, Pennsylvania German folk art symbols, Amish quilt designs, historic buildings, and the red rose symbol of Lancaster County.

"The dynamic mix and the blending of diverse cultural strands has woven a unique design into the patchwork quilt we call Lancaster County," says Donald B. Kraybill, provost at Messiah College in Grantham, Pennsylvania, and an authority on Old Order people and culture.

Lancaster County is indeed a patchwork quilt of small towns, well-preserved eighteenth- and nineteenth-century buildings, elegant and productive farms, Pennsylvania German food, Old Order settlements, antique shops, country auctions, natural areas, scenic sites, and historic churches. Few counties in the United States can match its quality of life, its colonial heritage, its historical firsts, its museums, its beautiful countryside, its bountiful agricultural production, its distin-

ctive Old Order culture, its small town living, its good and plenty food, and its inviting backroads. Other places claim some of those amenities; Lancaster County has them all.

Located in southcentral Pennsylvania, Lancaster County is sixty miles west of Philadelphia and one hundred miles north of Washington, D.C. With a population approaching 500,000, Lancaster is a metropolitan county with factories, shopping malls, office complexes, and suburban residential developments. It is the home of international corporations. Yet, it is also one of the most important farming counties in the United States.

Only a handful of American counties enjoys such national recognition as Lancaster County does. One reason is the concentration of separatist Old Order communities. Some four million tourists visit the area each year, making it a prime destination in the

Textile artist Donna Albert has designed this striking quilt that captures the diversity and heritage of Lancaster County. Entitled "Pennsylvania's Heartland," the patchwork quilt is a near-perfect snapshot of Lancaster County. (Photo © Keith Baum. Quilt courtesy of Murray Insurance Company of Lancaster City; quilt © 1990 by Donna Albert.)

Northeast. Their main interest is the Amish and Mennonites. The hardworking and plain-living Old Order people value faith, family, and farming. Old Order Amish and Old Order Mennonites use horse-and-buggy transportation, dress plainy, limit their formal education to eight grades in one-room schools, practice a conservative brand of Christianity, and have a lifestyle that conveys wholesome images of quieter and simpler times.

The Academy Award nominated movie *Witness* deepened the national awareness of the Lancaster County/Old Order Amish connection. Filmed in Lancaster County in the mid-1980s, the movie featured Harrison Ford as a Philadelphia police detective and Kelly McGillis as a young Amish widow. When their paths crossed as part of a murder investigation, they fell in love. Throughout the United States, moviegoers fell in love with *Witness* and Lancaster County.

The Amish and Mennonites are good neighbors and good citizens, and Lancaster County is fortunate to have them. But, they're just a piece of the goodly heritage and exceptional diversity of Lancaster County. There are many other patches in the Lancaster County quilt.

Lancaster County is dynamic and prosperous, with a nearly recession-proof economy centered on agriculture, tourism, manufacturing, and retail trade. Also, it's a big county with 950 square miles of land. Along with a handful of neighboring counties, it forms the popular Pennsylvania Dutch Country.

Because of its ideal East Coast location, its full-throttle economy, its good schools, and its pleasant, colorful countryside, Lancaster County is a magnet for commercial and residential growth. It has averaged an increase of 50,000 people in each of the last five decades. There's no reason to believe that rate of population growth will ease in the twenty-first century, as crowded suburban Philadelphia quickens its spread into Lancaster County.

The relentless development pressures are fraying the Lancaster County patchwork quilt.

Despite the growth trend that some people fear will eventually turn this special place into Anyplace USA, Lancaster County retains an enviable goodly heritage and appealing cultural diversity. Tom Daniels is the director of the Lancaster County Agricultural

A pair of Mennonite buggies clip-clop along a country road in eastern Lancaster County. The Plain People use horse-and-buggy transportation to visit, go shopping, and go to church. (Photo © Jerry Irwin)

FAMILY BUSINESS

Mom-and-pop businesses are a wonderful Lancaster County tradition. These small, family-owned businesses are often passed down from father to son. Case in point: the Bareville Woodcraft Company in Leola. Jacob Oberholtzer started the business across the street from his home thirty years ago. His wife, Anna, works in the office; his sons, Edward and J. Louis, are partners.

Lancaster County has countless little businesses along backcountry roads. They produce kitchen cabinets, lawn furniture, storage barns, wooden toys, cupolas, fasteners, and many other objects. These businesses employ ten to thirty workers. Quietly, they make quality products.

Most have a niche. Bareville Woodcraft Company's niche is steam bending wood. The company makes pieces for furniture, such as chairbacks, table rims, chair arms, and settee bows. It also makes carriage bows (the top framework of the buggy over which the fabric is stretched) for Amish buggies, and it used to make wooden wagon wheels, but the family sold off that component to an Amish businessman.

"I just wanted the challenge of having my own business," Jacob Oberholtzer says of why he began Bareville Woodcraft Company. And his business succeeded. The family sells its steam-bent pieces to furniture makers across the United States, including manufacturers of high-end furniture, such as Windsor and Queen Anne chairs. Buggy makers in Old Order communities buy the carriage bows.

The workers steam bend wood in vats heated to 240 degrees. "The steam softens the wood fibers and

The Bareville Woodcraft Company, one of hundreds of thriving Lancaster County small businesses, steam bends wood for furniture and for carriage bows on Old Order buggies. (Photo © Jerry Irwin)

makes the wood viable to bend," Jacob Oberholtzter says. Then, the steam-softened wood is put into presses and bent into shapes. The presses have forms on both sides, and the wood dries in the forms.

How many sales representatives does the business have to sell its products across the United States? The answer is none. "Our customers come to us," Jacob Oberholtzer says.

The Oberholtzers know in tradition-minded Lancaster County and in a rural, family-owned business quality counts.

Preserve Board, a government agency that purchases conservation easements from farmers to permanently preserve farmland. "Lancaster County has a conservative attitude, rooted in family and community," Daniels says. "This attitude says that small town life is honorable; belonging to a community is honorable. People who are born here tend to stay here. Extended families are remarkably close-knit. Although Lancaster County continues to experience rapid population growth, it has a strong sense of identity and pride in itself."

THE HISTORY OF LANCASTER COUNTY

To understand this identity and pride, it is necessary to go back to Lancaster County's beginnings. The

county was settled in the early 1700s by German, Swiss, Scots-Irish, English Quaker, and French Huguenot immigrants who were attracted to Pennsylvania because its Quaker founder William Penn promised religious liberty. They became farmers, doctors, fur traders, entrepreneurs, and artisans. Applying their skills and work ethic in a new land of opportunity, they thrived.

Though several religious groups settled in Lancaster County, the Protestant Pennsylvania Germans were dominant. They included Amish, Mennonites, Lutherans, Brethren, River Brethren, and Evangelical United Brethren. These groups profoundly influenced Lancaster County's character and personality. The Protestant Pennsylvania Germans valued

CONESTOGA WAGONS AND THE GOLDEN WEST

They were sturdy, bulky, and colorful. They were called the ships of inland commerce.

Conestoga wagons fueled colonial America's expansion, taking thousands of pioneers westward into the Ohio Valley. The wagons were first made in Lancaster County, and they got their name from the county's Conestoga River.

Immigrant Pennsylvania German artisans first built the wagons in the early 1700s. The vehicles were farm wagons that evolved into freight carriers. Arthur Reist, who lives in Lancaster County, wrote a book called *Conestoga Wagon: Masterpiece of the Blacksmith.* As he wrote: "The Conestoga wagon was a beautiful vehicle built by German wagon makers who adapted the construction and design to assure the teamster of reaching his destination through all kinds of weather and over the most adverse terrain."

Lancaster City was an important inland city in colonial times and a departure place for people heading west. Conestoga wagons carried most of the freight and people that moved westward over the Allegheny Mountains from 1775 to 1850.

The boat-shaped wagons put Lancaster on the map.

Both ends of the wagon were built higher than the middle. A high, rounded, white-canvas roof could be put on the vehicle, making it a covered wagon. Wheels with broad rims prevented the wagon from bogging down in mud. The high wheels could be

Conestoga wagons, like this one in front of the 1719 Hans Herr House, fueled America's westward expansion. They were first made in Lancaster County. (Photo © Keith Baum)

removed so the wagon could be used as a boat. Teams of four to six horses pulled a wagon.

Reist points out many Conestoga wagon drivers smoked thin, long cigars made from Lancaster County tobacco. People in western Pennsylvania and West Virginia dubbed the cigars "stogies," short for Conestoga.

Today, these wagons that played an important role in early American history are museum pieces and a symbol of Lancaster County.

Churchtown, a village in eastern Lancaster County, has the oldest Memorial Day parade in the United States. The village has celebrated the national holiday since 1866. (Photo © Jerry Irwin)

Lancaster County is anchored by family; many family roots date back to the early 1700s. Virtually all of Lancaster County's farms are family owned, just like the Larry Weaver farm where this tobacco is being planted. (Photo © Keith Baum)

honesty, hard work, close families, thrift, family-centered farming, conservatism, traditions, and stable communities. A peace-loving people, they became known as the "quiet in the land."

Lancaster County's borders were drawn in 1729, when it was carved out of neighboring Chester County. It's the fourth oldest of Pennsylvania's sixty-seven counties.

The city of Lancaster became the county seat. Its designers were influenced by Philadelphia, and, like the city of brotherly love, Lancaster has a grid street pattern and a center square. The first "King's Highway," a main artery between Philadelphia and the west, laid out in 1730–1735, led to the center of Lancaster, making the town's Penn Square an economic hub.

Because it was an early settlement, Lancaster County registered many American firsts. It has the oldest Amish community in America. The Strasburg Railroad is the country's oldest short-line, steam-powered railroad. The village of Churchtown has the oldest Memorial Day parade. Lancaster City, itself, boasts several national firsts, including the Fulton

Opera House, which is the oldest continuously operating theater; Lancaster Central Market, which is the oldest publicly owned and continuously operating farmers' market; and Demuth's Tobacco Shop, which is the oldest tobacco shop in the country.

Early Lancaster County's economy was driven by a few trades. The county was a center for rifle making in the Pennsylvania colony. The county's artisans produced the long-barrel Pennsylvania rifle, which was the most accurate firearm of its kind.

Also, early Lancaster County was a center of horology—the art of making timepieces. In the late 1700s and early 1800s, the county had more than 130 master clockmakers. Their specialty was tall-case, or grandfather, clocks, which are prized antiques today.

Even in colonial days, Lancaster County had a prosperous agricultural economy. Pennsylvania was the breadbasket of the colonies, and Lancaster County was the breadbasket of Pennsylvania. Wheat was its leading crop. Built along streams, water-powered grist mills were the center of social and business activity. Lancaster County had more than sixty mills before the

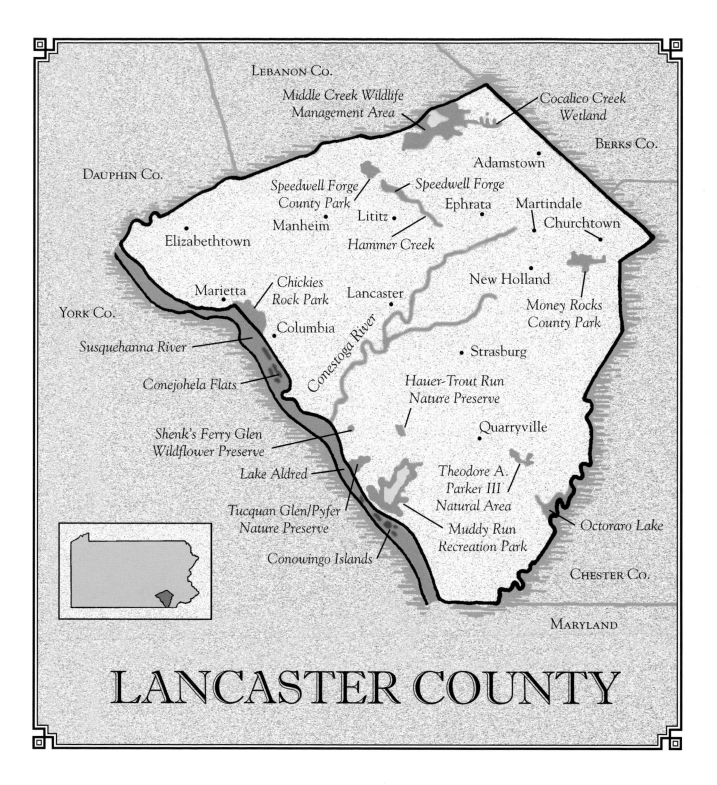

LANCASTER COUNTY

LEBANON CO.

Middle Creek Wildlife
Management Area

Cocalico Creek
Wetland

BERKS CO.

Adamstown

DAUPHIN CO.

Speedwell Forge
County Park

Speedwell Forge

Lititz

Ephrata

Martindale

Manheim

Churchtown

Elizabethtown

Hammer Creek

Chickies
Rock Park

New Holland

Marietta

Lancaster

Money Rocks
County Park

YORK CO.

Columbia

Susquehanna River

Conestoga River

Conejohela Flats

Strasburg

Hauer-Trout Run
Nature Preserve

Shenk's Ferry Glen
Wildflower Preserve

Quarryville

Lake Aldred

Theodore A.
Parker III
Natural Area

Tucquan Glen/Pyfer
Nature Preserve

Octoraro Lake

Muddy Run
Recreation Park

Conowingo Islands

CHESTER CO.

MARYLAND

Overleaf: As morning breaks, a balloon soars above the lush countryside near Strasburg in eastern Lancaster County. Lancaster County's farms provide a "sense of place." (Photo © Jerry Irwin)

Demuth's Tobacco Shop, located in downtown Lancaster City, is the oldest tobacco shop in the country, opening in 1770. Here, clerk Harold Rebman waits on customers. (Photo © Keith Baum)

Revolutionary War, and small, rural communities flourished around them.

Politically, Lancaster County also played a part in colonial America. In 1777, British troops forced the Continental Congress to flee Philadelphia. It met in Lancaster for a day, making the town, if only briefly, the capital of the newly independent United States. Lancastrian George Ross served on the Continental Congress and signed the Declaration of Independence. In 1789, the Lancaster County town of Columbia came within two votes of becoming the capital of the United States.

But Lancaster County's role in our nation's history isn't limited to Colonial times. Generations later, county native Thaddeus Stevens, serving as a dominant figure in the U.S. House of Representatives, championed freedom for slaves. In 1856, James Buchanan, of Lancaster, was elected president of the United States.

THE ESSENCE OF LANCASTER COUNTY

History is stitched into the Lancaster County quilt.

But, many other patches leap off its surface.

Patches like . . .

. . . religious heritage.

Historic Bangor Episcopal Church is in Churchtown. In May, when the carpet of green reappears, the church's minister and parishioners conduct an outdoor service called Rogation Day. It involves the blessing of "fields, seeds, animals, husbandmen, and wives" in hopes of a fruitful growing season. The church has carried on the service since the early 1750s.

Patches like . . .

. . . Old Order Lancaster County.

Samuel Stoltzfus is a dairy farmer, who shares the workload with his sons, Gideon and Issac. On the side, he makes gazebos and horseradish. He also belongs to the Old Order Amish Church. "Our church retains its original beliefs and worship modes," Stoltzfus says of his three-hundred-year-old religion.

Patches like . . .

. . . historic buildings and small towns.

Ephrata is a town of 12,200 residents in northern

Root's Country Market & Auction in Manheim displays the bounty of Lancaster County's agricultural diversity. Lancaster County farmers raise pigs, cows, cattle, sheep, and chickens. Also, they grown hay, corn, wheat, barley, fruits, and vegetables. (Photo © Jerry Irwin)

Lancaster County. In downtown Ephrata, Sprecher's Hardware Store dates back to the 1860s as a business. People call it the everything store because it has everything, including a 1912 cage-style elevator. Ephrata's neighborhoods contain well-built late nineteenth- and earlier twentieth-century homes that make the community seem clean and safe.

Like Donna Albert's "Pennsylvania's Heartland" quilt, the Lancaster County quilt is loaded with patches. But what binds them together? Four strong threads:

> A sense of place.
> A sense of community.
> A sense of family.
> A sense of tradition.

A SENSE OF PLACE

Farmland defines Lancaster County; two-thirds of Lancaster County's 600,000 acres is farmland. Farms convey Lancaster County's sense of place.

Lancaster County is located on the Piedmont plateau, a transition area between the Atlantic coastal plain and the Appalachian Mountains. The county is a broad limestone valley of rolling terrain with deep fertile soils, and this gift of good land has made Lancaster County the Garden Spot of America. The county is one of America's most well-known working landscapes.

Lancaster County has 4,700 family-owned farms. The farms average eighty-five acres, but these small farms produce big results. In fact, Lancaster County is the most productive non-irrigated farming county in the United States. Its agriculture is diverse, ranking among the national leaders in poultry, eggs, and milk.

Donald Robinson has worked with Lancaster County farmers for thirty years. Robinson is the administrator of the Lancaster County Soil Conservation District, a government agency that works to maintain water quality and prevent soil erosion. He knows what makes Lancaster County agriculture so great. "The soil, the people, the location, the climate,

A NEW OUTLOOK ON LIFE

Each summer Lancaster County families welcome hundreds of needy New York City youngsters into their homes as part of the Fresh Air Fund. This boy seems excited about playing with his first little pig. (Photo © Jerry Irwin)

Lancaster County has a big heart.

That big heart shines through every summer when hundreds of families host needy children from New York City.

The families participate in The Fresh Air Fund, which has provided free summer vacations to more than 1.6 million disadvantaged children since 1877. Lancaster County families have helped out since 1891. The county is one of the agency's top areas for placing children.

The program is simple. Boys and girls, ages six to eighteen, stay for two weeks with a host family. The families are not paid; they just want to share their homes with inner-city youngsters.

The Fresh Air Fund is a wonderful tradition in Lancaster County, especially among farm families. Many families have helped children for three generations. In a typical year, Lancaster County hosts four hundred youngsters.

Barbara Horst, of Akron, is the coordinator of the Lancaster County program. Her family has hosted children for nearly thirty years. "My summer wouldn't feel right without giving children a new outlook on life," she says.

the agribusiness infrastructure, and the diversity of livestock and crops are all part of it," he said. "But, the most important ingredient is our heritage. It's pride—pride in our farms and pride in being a farmer. Heritage is something alive, vibrant, and passed on."

He got it right.

Lancaster County's farming heritage—the tidy farmhouses with their large flower and vegetable gardens, the perfectly contoured fields, the golden sunlight cutting across tall fields of corn, rolling farm terrain, freshly painted barns stuffed with hay and straw, the large number of 200-year-old farms run by descendants of the original owners, the bountiful harvests, and the careful hands-on stewardship of the good earth—distinguishes its agriculture and produces a land ethic unmatched in the United States.

Lancaster County's agricultural landscape is a beautiful work of art.

Viewed from the ground or the air, the pretty and productive farms proclaim: "This is the heart of Lancaster County."

A SENSE OF COMMUNITY

"I am my brother's keeper."

Lucy Oberholtzer was almost finished milking cows in the barn near Blue Ball in eastern Lancaster County. It was the evening milking. Her son, Brian, had climbed up a ladder to get feed for the cows when he saw a farm family's worst fear. "Fire! Fire!" he yelled.

Edwin Oberholtzer, Lucy's husband, was on the other side of the barn. He heard the commotion and ran for a fire extinguisher, but he soon realized the only thing he could do was to get the cows out. The family saved its fifty-cow herd, and no one was hurt. But, the 125-year-old barn was lost to the flames.

Lancaster County is growing in population, and the population increase is changing the landscape and bringing newcomers into neighborhoods. Still, Lancaster County has retained its sense of community. Nothing illustrates this better than how the neighbors rallied to the Oberholtzers in their hour of need. They had a barn raising.

Barn raisings are common in Lancaster County. They are a routine part of community life in the region, especially among Anabaptist believers, such as the Oberholtzers. They interpret the Bible in a literal way. And the Bible says this about mutual aid in Galatians 6:10: "Therefore, as we have opportunity, let us do good to all people, especially to those who belong to the family of believers."

Barn raisings are a common expression of rural Lancaster County's neighborly spirit. When a fire destroyed Edwin and Lucy Oberholtzer's dairy barn outside of Blue Ball, the community cleaned up the debris and raised a new barn in a matter of days. (Photo © Keith Baum)

The day after the fire was out, volunteers cleaned up the debris. As the debris was removed, head carpenter Aaron Horst organized the first phase of the barn raising, building a foundation. Edwin Oberholtzer recalls it this way: "Neighbors contacted Mr. Horst. You got to have a lead man. Everybody went to him. He told them what to do—where to lay block and where to dig footers. He ordered all the stuff and got it here."

Once the foundation was finished, which took just a few days, the barn raising began. Some 150 men with hammers, saws, and other tools built a new barn in less than two days. When it was time to eat, women had tables of homemade food ready. Grocery stores donated provisions. Everyone was a volunteer; helping out a neighbor in need was just something that had to be done.

And ten days after the fire, the Oberholtzers had a new barn. "It's almost more than what words can explain," Oberholtzer says. "It's unbelievable how many people showed up to help. Our community has shown how much good can happen when we work together."

A SENSE OF FAMILY

It was a wonderful May day when eighty people gathered for the annual meeting and reunion of the Eby Family Association at Overly's Grove outside New Holland. They enjoyed fun, food, and fellowship, but most importantly, they celebrated family.

Lancaster County has a sense of family; family has played a strong role in its history. If the late 1700s had a telephone book to compare to the late 1990s, there would be an amazing constancy in names. Surnames such as Brubaker, Weaver, Good, Martin, Hess, Sensenig, and Burkholder would dominate the listings in both books.

Lancaster County's conservative values sustain family life and community stability. Genealogy is a passion. Family heirlooms are passed down from generation to generation; family Bibles are cherished.

But reunions best express Lancaster County's sense of family.

"Family reunions bind together acceptance, comfort, accountability, and warmth," says author and Lancaster County resident Joanne Hess Siegrist.

In Lancaster County, family reunions celebrate roots. And, those roots go back to the early 1700s.

In 1992, Christian Eaby organized the Eby Family Association (several different spellings of the Eby surname have developed through the generations). Fourteen people met in his home, which was the original Eby House of Lancaster County, built by Theodorus Eby, who came to America some time around 1715. Built in the 1720s, the stone farmhouse lies south of New Holland. Theodorus Eby is believed to be buried in the graveyard across from the house.

The Eby Family Association has accomplished plenty. It has fixed up the family graveyard and used donated funds to restore the Eby family Bible, which was printed in 1596. It publishes a newsletter. It holds annual reunions. And, its membership has grown to three hundred families.

This reunion was a success, attracting people from ten states. They ate, watched a slide show about the restoration of the family Bible, and had an all-around good time. Charles and Reta Abee traveled the longest distance, driving 1,500 miles from Texas. Eighty-year-old Zona Eby Navelle was the oldest, coming from New York State.

Christian is Theodorus Eby's great-great-great-great-great-great grandson and now serves as the association's president. "Reunions show real family values," he says.

A SENSE OF TRADITION

On a picture-perfect June Sunday morning, hundreds of worshipers gathered inside Zion Evangelical Lutheran Church in Manheim.

Manheim is an old Lancaster County town founded in 1762 under the leadership of "Baron" Henry William Stiegel, a man of considerable stature in colonial Pennsylvania. He was a wealthy iron baron and maker of lovely glassware, and he became a benefactor to Manheim.

Zion Evangelical Lutheran Church is also old, almost as old as Manheim itself. The church celebrated its 225th anniversary in 1997, having been founded in 1772, four years before the signing of the Declaration of Independence. Located in the center of town, the church is a handsome brick building with stained-glass windows. The present building, built in 1891, is the congregation's third house of worship.

Zion Evangelical Lutheran Church is known as "The Red Rose Church." The red rose is the symbol of Lancaster County, but the church is known as "The Red Rose Church" for another reason. Henry William Stiegel, Zion Evangelical Lutheran Church, and the red rose are forever linked because of Stiegel's generosity.

A devout Lutheran, Stiegel had a chapel in his home. In 1772, Stiegel and his wife, Elizabeth, "leased" to Manheim Lutherans a plot of ground to build a church. The down payment for the land was a nominal five shillings and "in the month of June yearly forever hereafter the rent of one red rose if the same shall be lawfully demanded." Stiegel loved music and beauty, but he especially loved red roses.

On the second Sunday in June, in a special ceremony as part of the regular worship service, the church pays the rent of one red rose to a selected Stiegel descendant. The Festival of the Red Rose has been part of the service since 1892.

A sense of tradition is a thread that binds together the Lancaster County patchwork quilt. Lancaster is a conservative county that respects its past. Lancaster County cherishes traditions, and few of them are better than the Red Rose Festival.

During the festival, the church is decorated with roses, and as worshipers enter, they each receive a rose, which they then put in a basket at the altar. Many of the roses used in the service, including the one presented to the Stiegel heir, are grown and harvested on church grounds. The service is conducted against the backdrop of the beautiful Stiegel stained-glass window, which depicts a red rose at its center.

Rod Frey, Jr., is in charge of the festival committee.

Opposite top: Reunions recapture Lancaster County's family roots, which date to the early 1700s. After having a reunion, members of the Eby Family Association posed for a picture outside the original Eby House near New Holland. The stone farmhouse was built in the 1720s. (Photo © Keith Baum)

Opposite bottom: Zion Evangelical Lutheran Church in Manheim has had an annual Festival of the Red Rose for more than a hundred years. The June program celebrates the church's heritage. In the church's rose garden, children are photographed with Baron Henry William Steigel likeness Robert McCabe. (Photo © Keith Baum)

"This is a way of showing our thanks and gratitude for what Henry William Stiegel gave to the first Lutheran congregation in Manheim," he says.

The program begins with the reading of the deed. When the church paid its rent in 1997, attorney Andrea Eveler Stanley represented the congregation. She gave the flower to Cynthia Fager Rawling, a ninth-generation descendant of Stiegel. Both signed the Red Rose Receipt Book, making the rent payment official. The recipient lives in Pennsylvania. Her father, who lives in New Jersey, received a red rose in 1987. And, an aunt, who lives in Arizona, took home a rose in 1977. Other recipients include Millicent McNally Cooper, of Florida, who was honored in 1995, and the Reverend Russell Stiegel, Jr., of South Carolina, who accepted the red rose in 1976. "To me, this is a very unique tradition," Mrs. Fager Rawling says.

When Zion Evangelical Lutheran Church marked its 200th anniversary, it published a historical booklet that contained a poem written by Anna Balmer Myers. The last stanza reads:

"So much beauty Stiegel gave the world;
    The colored glass like jewels that God made,
The church that pays a yearly one red rose—
    These are rich legacies that never fade."

At least not in Lancaster County.

Lancaster County has a sense of place best expressed by its pretty and productive farms: farming, always farming.

Lancaster County has a sense of community best expressed by a barn raising: I am my brother's keeper.

Lancaster County has a sense of family best shown at a reunion: Roots.

Lancaster County has a sense of tradition: Lasting roots.

These senses make Lancaster County a special place.

Three Old Order Amish boys bundle up against the cold and wind near their one-room school. Though it's winter, one youngster is wearing a warm-weather straw hat. Traditional plain clothes are a signature of Old Order Lancaster County. (Photo © Keith Baum)

THE RELIGIOUS HERITAGE OF LANCASTER COUNTY

PAUL HURST STOOD next to a table inside a big trailer, placing yellow labels with black letters on cans of beef. The labels read: Food for Relief—In the Name of Christ. They carry the logo of the Mennonite Central Committee (MCC), whose international headquarters are in the Lancaster County town of Akron.

Lancaster County was founded by European immigrants who came to America in the 1700s to escape the persecution of state churches and to enjoy the religious liberty that Quaker William Penn promised with his Holy Experiment in the colony of Pennsylvania. Penn was a supreme idealist, who wanted a colony where various nationalities would have the freedom to worship without fear of persecution from civil authorities. His experiment in tolerance had a lasting effect on many parts of Pennsylvania, and today, a rich and diverse religious heritage survives in Lancaster County. In a book published in 1844, historian I. Daniel Rupp wrote: "If diversity of creeds or multiplicity of religious

---

Main photo: *Lancaster County has dozens of historic churches with classic looks. Bangor Episcopal Church, which dates to 1722, is on the National Register of Historic Places. This is an interior view showing the ornate wooden beams of the present stone church. (Photo © Keith Baum)*

Inset: *This rural Lancaster County roadside sign mixes business and religion. Signs like this one, which often cite Bible verses, dot the rural landscape. (Photo © Keith Baum)*

sects serve as a standard of deep toned piety and Christian benevolence, then may the people of Lancaster County lay claim to a goodly share. For there is no place upon earth . . . that counts more denominations than Lancaster."

The Mennonites are a very important part of this religious diversity. Swiss Mennonites were the earliest settlers in Lancaster County, arriving in 1710. During the eighteenth century, more than twenty Mennonite churches were founded in the county, including one of the oldest meetinghouses in America, constructed in 1719. A private residence, the building was used for worship. Today it is a museum called the Hans Herr House, and the structure is the oldest building in Lancaster County.

MCC is the cooperative relief, service, and development agency of the North American Mennonite and Brethren in Christ churches. The MCC is part of the modern Mennonite Church, a mainstream branch, though many Old Order Mennonites participate in the canning effort. The MCC began in 1920, sending food and volunteers, "In the Name of Christ," to war-torn Russia. MCC's philosophy is rooted in the Anabaptist faith, which believes in a free church separate from the state and joined voluntarily by adults professing their faith through baptism. Mennonites renounce the use of violence and force, and they seek to carry Christ's message to hurting people throughout the world.

Jesus Christ called on his followers to visit the sick, clothe the naked, and feed the hungry.

Feed the hungry. That's what Hurst and others did as participants in MCC's meat canning program at the John F. Martin & Sons, Inc. meat packing plant in northern Lancaster County. The plant owners support the MCC project, allowing the volunteers to debone meat inside the plant and process it in a nearby canning trailer. The project allows Christian believers to practice their faith in fellowship with friends and neighbors. Working with joyful hearts, some nine hundred people were volunteers in the mid-March meat canning effort. For five days, they cut up, cooked, packed, labeled, and stored cans of beef chunks. They filled 23,000 cans, or nearly 20 tons.

"It's a blessing to us," Hurst says.

The canning trailer travels to other communities in the United States and Canada. The organization also distributes the beef cans to local churches and charitable organizations in countries such as Bosnia-Herzegovina, Haiti, Laos, Nicaragua, Russia, and the

St. Stephen United Church of Christ is a landmark church in New Holland. The 1799 brick church is one of the most elegant meetinghouse-type churches in Lancaster County. (Photo © Keith Baum)

United States. The meat is served in hospitals, nursing homes, schools, shelters for abandoned children, and prisons.

Tom Daniels, the director of the Lancaster County Agricultural Preserve Board, comes in contact with many people through the course of his work. He has lived in several parts of the country, and he has a good read on Lancaster County. "The people in Lancaster County are more religious than in most other places," Daniels says. "But, they are people who live their religion. 'Do unto others' is a motto that applies in everyday living."

The MCC meat canning project exemplifies this "do unto others" value. MCC has nine hundred workers serving in fifty countries. Because of its size and international reach, MCC is an important example of Lancaster County's religious heritage. There are many others.

The religious heritage of the county has shaped its character and personality as much as the fertile farmland, providing a sense of tolerance, a conservative attitude toward life, a stable community, a respect for tradition, and a strong faith.

When Lancaster County was formed in 1729 out of neighboring Chester County, it already had eleven congregations of the Brethren, Mennonite, Society of Friends, Presbyterian, and German Reformed churches. In the 1700s, nearly seventy-five churches were started.

Lancaster County had ten Presbyterian churches founded in the 1700s. One of the grandest is the Donegal Presbyterian Church outside of Mount Joy. Built as a log church in 1721 by Scots-Irish immigrants,

A PECULIAR PEOPLE

More than one hundred years ago, American illustrator and writer Howard Pyle did an article for Harper's magazine called "A Peculiar People: A Tale of the Ephrata Cloister." That was the perfect title for one of Lancaster County's most unusual social groups, a community that left behind magnificent buildings and important pieces of history.

The Ephrata Cloister was one of America's earliest communal societies. Housed in a collection of Germanic-style buildings, the community of religious zealots practiced an austere lifestyle that stressed spiritual and mystical goals. Also known for its original music and artwork, the Ephrata Cloister was an important center for printing and publishing in colonial Pennsylvania.

Ten of its original buildings have been brilliantly restored to recreate the historical communal village. Now it's a state-owned museum and national historic landmark.

The commune was an example of an early American counterculture. Founded by Conrad Beissel, an enigmatic religious fanatic, the cloister attracted true believers. They led a life of discipline and self-denial, which included celibacy, in an effort to achieve a oneness with God.

The cloister is located along a busy road in the

During the Christmas season, candles are placed in windows of the Sister's House, known as "the Saron," at the Ephrata Cloister. The building, which was built in 1743, is part of the museum. (Photo © Keith Baum)

town of Ephrata. Cars zoom by, but it breathes a stoic serenity that visitors sense. The modern world disappears; the old world of the Ephrata Cloister appears. It is as if the cloister is saying: "Be still" for "Lo, from the stillness of Zion proceedeth the brightness of God."

the church is one of the oldest Presbyterian churches in the United States. The present church, which was built in 1740, is on the National Register of Historic Places.

The village of Churchtown has a church on the National Register of Historic Places, too. Welsh immigrants founded Bangor Episcopal Church in 1722 when Churchtown was a prosperous iron-producing community. The present stone church was built in 1830. An example of early Gothic Revival architecture, Bangor Church is the oldest inland Episcopal church in the United States. More than three hundred tombstones are in the adjoining graveyard. The oldest dates to 1741, bearing the name of Mary Edwards, who died at age three.

St. Mary's Catholic Church in Lancaster City traces its history back to 1741. It is the mother church of Catholicism in Lancaster County and the fourth oldest Catholic church in the United States. The

Volunteers work in the Mennonite Central Committee meat canning program. Workers put their religious faith into practice preparing cans of beef for needy people throughout the world. (Photo © Keith Baum)

THE PUTZ

The Lititz Moravian Church's trombone choir and Christmas season lovefeast each go back hundreds of years. Another honored church tradition is the putz. Putz, which is pronounced "puts," is a home display of scenery and figures showing the story of the Christ child's nativity. The term "putz" was taken from an archaic definition of a German word, *putzen*, which meant to decorate a church. The Moravians, who migrated to America in the seventeenth century and settled in Lititz, brought the putz tradition with them.

In colonial Lititz, families began to gather natural materials as early as September for the diorama. After Thanksgiving, fathers constructed their putz. The putz was unveiled on Christmas Eve, and the children narrated the story of the nativity. At Christmastime, families went "putzing," visiting their neighbors to view their displays.

Today, the construction of home putzes has declined. But the Lititz Moravian Church displays a volunteer-built putz. It is arranged in a sixteen-by-six-foot canopy stage. To create a natural look, the volunteers place twelve illuminated scenes among live moss and plants, and the hand-painted sky contains lighted stars. The putz figures and scenery are all handmade and hand-painted by church members. The

Carol Baum, and her son, David, enjoy the putz at the Lititz Moravian Church. A putz is a display of scenery and figures that show the story of the Christ child's nativity. (Photo © Keith Baum)

church pastors narrate each scene for the congregation, while the church choir performs almost all the songs.

Suzanne Snyder is in charge of erecting the putz. A church member, she takes her work seriously. "This is the real story of Christmas," she says.

Right: *Reverend Thomas McKinnon, Jr. wears a Green Bay Packers cheesehead hat during his children's sermon, passing religion from generation to generation in an entertaining way. The service at historic Donegal Presbyterian Church was on Super Bowl Sunday in 1998. (Photo © Keith Baum)*
Opposite: *A couple is married at St. Mary's Catholic Church in Lancaster City by the Reverend Bernardo Pistone. The three-altar church is the fourth oldest Catholic church in the United States; the original log church was completed in 1742. (Photo © Keith Baum)*

church has three altars, a magnificent organ, marble statues, frescoes of the twelve apostles, and breath-takingly beautiful stained-glass windows. "I pray that when you visit this ancient Holy Place, you have met the God of love and fidelity," says the church's Father Bernardo Pistone.

Another example of Lancaster County's religious heritage is the Society of Friends, or Quakers. In the 1700s, six Quaker meetings, or congregations, were started in Lancaster County, and several are still part of the area's religious landscape. In Little Britain

Opposite top: The Moravian Church is tradition-minded. The trombone choir of the Lititz Moravian Church, begun in 1771, plays on church greens for the Sunday service after Christmas and at a few other times throughout the year. (Photo © Keith Baum)

Opposite bottom: Quaker meetings are known for their simplicity of structure. This is the 1803 Eastland Meeting in southern Lancaster County. (Photo © Jerry Irwin)

Township in southern Lancaster County, the handsome stone building that houses the Eastland Meeting survives. Eastland Preparative Meeting of the Society of Friends was established in 1796 and held its first meetings in a schoolhouse. The present structure was built in 1803.

Lutherans founded four churches in 1730 alone, including Holy Trinity Lutheran Church in Lancaster City. The present church's 195-foot steeple was the second tallest in North America when it was completed in 1794.

Lancaster County's old churches are exceptional examples of architecture and tradition. One church complex stands out on both counts: the Moravian Square in Lititz. The Lititz Moravian Church was organized in 1749; the present church was built in 1787. "The Moravian Church is a very traditional church," says archivist Jean Doherty. Those traditions include the Moravian star, the trombone choir, and the

"FEED MY FLOCK"

Lancaster County is blessed with the gift of good people and the gift of good land. Those gifts find their clearest expression in Paul Beyer.

For more than thirty-five years, Paul Beyer has collected donated bread, melons, corn, eggs, meats, and other foods from Lancaster County farmers and businesses. Once a week, he makes a six-hour round-trip from his Rothsville home to the Bowery Mission in New York City.

Jesus said: "Feed my flock."

The flock at the Bowery Mission are poor men in need of food and hope. The Mission gives them hope, and Lancaster County gives them food. In fact, Lancaster County gives the Bowery Mission two-thirds of the food it needs to serve between 500 and 600 meals a day.

"In the summertime, I'm taking three-quarters of a ton of food a week," Beyer says.

When he started, Beyer was a volunteer. He had a good-paying job repairing furniture; then mission officials asked him to work for them. He took a pay cut (nearly half his salary) and accepted the offer because he believed the Lord wanted him to help feed His flock. Now, Beyer drives around Lancaster County

with his Bowery Mission truck. He is a soft-spoken man doing the Lord's work. He has done this for 36 years and has traveled more than 600,000 miles on his mission.

Beyer belongs to the Millport Mennonite Church. Mennonites are Christians whose Anabaptist beliefs instruct them to put their faith into practice helping needy people "In His name."

"I like what I'm doing," Beyer says. "When you see the smiles on those men's faces. . . . They come and give you hugs and say 'I love you.' People trust me with the food I take up there."

Beyer is in his late 60s. He's not slowing down, but he can't go on forever. "I plan to keep at it until the Lord finds someone to take my place," he says. "Now, nobody wants to do it. When the Lord wants me to quit, He'll have somebody to take my place."

Above: Paul Beyer picks up fresh vegetables from a Lancaster County farm. He takes local goods to the Bowery Mission in New York City to feed needy men. (Photo © Keith Baum)

lovefeast.

Every year during Advent, Moravians hang a star in their churches and display a star on their porches; in the chancel of the Lititz Moravian Church there is an impressive 110-point star. The white Moravian star is a many-pointed orb of light, which, it is believed, strikes rays of peace and hope into every heart.

The trombone choir—which now has trumpets, cornets, French horns, and tubas, in addition to trombones—began in 1771 as a slide trombone group. It sometimes plays on the church greens, announcing all festival days and other important church happenings. On Easter, the Moravian musicians rouse Lititz with tunes before dawn. At Christmas, they accompany church carolers. The trombone choir is one of the oldest instrumental worship choirs in the oldest of the Protestant denominations, the Moravian Church having pre-Reformation roots in the 1400s.

The lovefeast is a religious service done almost all in music. The first lovefeast was in 1756, and the long tradition incorporates the trombone choir and the Moravian star in a beautiful ceremony where few words are spoken. Worshipers enter the church to the chorales of the choir. When the congregation is inside, lights are extinguished and the choir sings *Stille Nacht, Heilige Nacht,* "Silent Night" in German. As the choir sings, the Moravian star brightens, reaching a brilliant intensity by the final refrain. After "Silent Night," servers distribute buns and coffee while the choir and congregation sing hymns. Servers then distribute lighted candles to the worshipers, who eventually hold more than 600 aloft. The service concludes with a benediction, silent prayer, and organ postlude.

St. Stephen United Church of Christ is in New Holland. The building dates to 1799, and the brick church is one of the most elegant meetinghouse-style churches in Lancaster County, with its commanding 120-foot tower. Church leaders believe the design was influenced by the work of architect Sir Christopher Wren who designed scores of churches in England in the late 1600s and early 1700s. Simplicity and graceful structural relationships, as evidenced in St. Stephen Church, distinguish his work.

The Old Order Amish and Old Order Mennonite churches of Lancaster County—the plain, separatist churches—are the pillars of the county's religious heritage. The Old Order people are pious Christians of German ancestry, and religion is the axis of Old Order life. The Old Order stresses simple church practices, a ministry exclusively performed by men, a ministry chosen by lot for life, and a conservative brand of Christianity. They value tradition over change. Old Order Lancaster County is the basis for the next chapter.

William Penn founded Pennsylvania as a Holy Experiment. More than any Pennsylvania county, Lancaster County stands out as an example of what he sought to do: establish a land of religious tolerance. "The uniqueness of Lancaster County is its good mixture of mainstream people and a wide variety of separatist groups," says farmer Willis Kilheffer. "This community then and now is probably the last evidence of William Penn's Holy Experiment illustrating the answer to his question, 'Can people of various beliefs and origins live together peacefully?'"

In Lancaster County, they can.

Historic Coleman Chapel is located in northern Lancaster County. In 1874, George and Deborah Coleman added the sandstone chapel to an existing meetinghouse. The pews reverse so worshipers can face the east doors of the church and view the sunrise during the Easter service. (Photo © Keith Baum)

THE OLD ORDERS
OF LANCASTER COUNTY

IT'S SUNDAY MORNING — church time in Old Order Lancaster County.

David Fisher's Amish farm is south of New Holland, a town in eastern Lancaster County. This Sunday, the church service is inside his farmhouse.

Twenty-five Amish families, a total of 160 people, attend the service at David Fisher's house. The men, women, and children of the congregation are Fisher's neighbors; they all live within two or so miles of his dairy farm in the lush Mill Creek Valley. Families arrive by horse-and-buggy. In one buggy, little children press against the back window. Walking side by side, teenage girls appear in their dark blue church dresses, offset by the white of the capes on their backs and the prayer coverings on their heads.

As church tradition requires, men and women, boys and girls enter the farmhouse separately. They sit on backless benches—men and boys on one side

Main photo: *With three passengers, an Amish horse-and-buggy rides down a rural southern Lancaster County road. An Amish farmhouse and farm buildings are in the background. (Photo © Jerry Irwin)*

Inset: *The spring auction in Gordonville is called a mud sale for obvious reasons. Two Amish men take a break from the events and lean against a buggy to chat. (Photo © Keith Baum)*

of the room, women and girls on the other side.

The Old Order Amish Church is a conservative branch of Christianity and a successful separatist culture. Many other American churches more readily embrace change, adopting new ideas in liturgy, organization, and, in some cases, beliefs. Not the Amish church. It is deeply rooted in the past and happy about it. Its services are the same today—same songbook, same communion practices, and same wedding ceremonies—as they were hundreds of years ago. In a time when cultural change races ahead, this is nothing short of a miracle.

In the Amish church, only men are ministers. They're picked by lot for life, as the Amish believe the Bible commands. The service is conducted in German.

The Old Order Amish worship in homes. David Luthy is a writer and editor for Pathway Publishers, an Old Order Amish publishing house in Ontario, Canada. Luthy speaks of the importance of having church in homes. In his words: "In Amish society, 'church' is people not a building. Gathering for worship services in our homes best exemplifies the glue which holds Amish society together—fellowship. As the first notes of the opening hymn float through our home on Sunday, we forget all the work to get the house ready and rejoice in the special feeling of fellowship—the 'church' has once again gathered at our home."

Inside the farmhouse, the worshipers open their songbook called the *Ausbund*, or, as the Amish would say, "the thick book." The *Ausbund*, dating from 1564, is the oldest songbook used in congregational singing in the world. *Ausbund* means selection or anthology. It has no musical notes; the tunes, memorized in childhood while attending services, are sung a cappella. The worshipers sing very slowly, creating music much like a Gregorian chant. The words break the morning quiet: "O God, our Father, Thee we praise."

Persecuted by the state and churches in Europe for their religious beliefs more than three hundred years ago, the Amish sought religious liberty in America. The immigrants came to Pennsylvania in the mid-1700s, making Lancaster County the homeland of the

Amish church. Today, there are twenty thousand Amish people living in Lancaster County.

Lancaster County is a patchwork quilt. Its centerpiece—its most famous patch—is the Old Order Amish.

But, the Amish are only one of the Old Order churches that constitute the Plain People culture. Several Old Order Mennonite churches, the River Brethren Church, and other religious groups make up Old Order Lancaster County. More than forty thousand people in Lancaster County—about 8 percent of the population—identify with Old Order churches and related groups.

The Old Order churches, among themselves, differ. Unlike the Amish, the Old Order Mennonites worship in meetinghouses. Lancaster County has twenty meetinghouses, including the Pike Church outside of Ephrata. "Team Mennonites"—those who use horses and buggies for transportation—worship at the Pike Church. Their 160-year-old meetinghouse is a simple, plain, white wooden building.

The Old Order Mennonites sing from a different songbook, as well. They use the *Unpartheyisches Gesang-Buch*, which was first printed in 1804. *Unpartheyisches Gesang-Buch* means, literally, impartial songbook, a hymnal suitable for any Protestant group to use.

In addition to having different songbooks and places of worship, there are other differences between the Old Order Amish and Old Order Mennonites. Amish men have beards; Mennonite men do not. Amish have gray buggy tops, while Mennonites have black. Amish use no electricity from utilities; most Mennonite homes are connected to power company lines. Amish don't have telephones in their homes; most Mennonites do.

The Old Order Mennonites differ among themselves in many ways. Groffdale Church members have motorized steel-wheel tractors, but they use horse-and-buggy transportation. Their church leaders limit technology on farms. The Weaverland Church members, on the other hand, have cars—but the cars can only be black. Often, even the bumpers are painted black, leading some to refer to this group as the "black

Above: *Old Order Mennonites worship at meetinghouses, which are framed churches. These buggies are parked under trees at a meetinghouse north of New Holland. (Photo © Keith Baum)*
Opposite: *Early on, Amish youngsters are taught to respect their elders and the rich heritage of their forefathers. Respect for both is fundamental to the Old Order credo. (Photo © Keith Baum)*

LOVINA'S STITCHERY

Ooh and aah. That's what visitors do when they step into Lovina Beiler's quilt shop outside of Strasburg. They ooh and aah over her gorgeous handmade quilts. Lovina's Stitchery is one of Lancaster County's best quilt shops.

Lovina Beiler belongs to the Old Order Amish Church. Quilting is very popular in Lancaster County, and Amish women are especially dedicated quilters. Mothers teach their daughters the art and skills of quilt making. Families and friends go to quilting bees where women sit around a quilting rack to stitch. Quilting bees are a celebration of needle and thread. And they're a pleasurable social event.

Many quilt shops are nice but Lovina's Stitchery is extra nice. Her little family business sets high standards when it comes to picking colors, selecting designs, and doing the quilting.

She sells quilts for beds, wallhanging quilts, and craft objects, such as faceless Amish dolls and potholders.

"Owning a quilt shop means working with people, helping them find what they are looking for and then be proud of what they bought," Mrs. Beiler says.

Above: *Naomi Stoltzfus stitches a quilt at Lovina's Stitchery near Strasburg. Lovina Beiler owns the quilt shop that sells attractive quilts and crafts. (Photo © Jerry Irwin)*

Selling spring homegrown strawberries and learning, that's what this Amish boy is doing near Strasburg. (Photo © Keith Baum)

bumper church." The church has virtually no restrictions on farm technology.

A third, smaller Old Order group, the River Brethren, live mainly in western Lancaster County. Unlike the Old Order Amish and Old Order Mennonites, who limit their children's formal education to eight grades, River Brethren allow youngsters to go to high school. The church's services, which are in homes or schools, are in English. The River Brethren baptize by immersion in water.

LEFTOVER VALUES

Despite their differences, the churches share a patchwork of Old Order values—a common credo.

In an intriguing way, Phares Hurst, a farmer and barn-painter who belongs to the Old Order Mennonite Church, sums up the essence of the credo this way: "Like an island in a sea of encroaching modern pressures, we have leftover values."

Leftover values that show respect for elders and forefathers.

Leftover values that stress cooperation for the good of the community instead of competition for the good of the individual.

And, leftover values that produce strong families without divorce, where mothers stay home to raise children, and where fathers provide loving guidance.

"The upside-down values of Old Order life esteem tradition as much as change, lift communal goals above personal ones, prefer work over consumption and place personal sacrifice on par with pleasure," says Donald B. Kraybill, the provost at Messiah College and author of several books on the Amish and other Old Order groups.

The Old Order people descend from the Anabaptist movement of sixteenth-century Europe, a tributary of the Protestant Reformation. Anabaptists believe in voluntary adult baptism, the separation of church and state, the rejection of force, and living the Golden Rule. The Old Orders—the most conservative of Lancaster County's Anabaptist churches—are thriving and growing despite existing in the bosom of modern pressures that might tempt members to leave for liberal churches.

Old Order Lancaster County is about leftover values.

The core leftover value is obedience to God's Word. What separates the Plain People from other Christians is their strict interpretation of the Scriptures, the application of biblical values to their everyday life,

and their reluctance to be swept along by popular cultural and religious trends. "The Plain People have taken many Scriptures literally, which other Christians have spiritualized, explained away, or ignored," says writer Stephen Scott, a member of the River Brethren Church who has written several books on Old Order subjects. "Nonswearing of oaths, the forbiddance of divorce and remarriage, feet washing, the holy kiss, uncut hair, and head coverings for women have been retained despite societal pressures to give up these practices. The Plain People believe that the Christian life is one of self-denial and humility, as exemplified by their supreme role model, Jesus Christ."

Old Order Mennonite historian and farmer Amos Hoover points out that an Old Order person believes "in the hard sayings of the Bible" in addition to the basic teachings. The "hard sayings" such as

Love your enemies. Matthew 5:44

No suing or countersuing. Matthew 5:40

Anyone who looks at a woman lustfully has already committed adultery with her in his heart. Matthew 5:28. Therefore, the body must be covered to prevent lust.

Many biblical verses explain the Old Order credo. But, Romans 12:2 does it the best: "And be not conformed to this world; but be ye transformed by the renewing of your mind."

Old Order families are rooted on farms, though, increasingly, adult men are working in nonfarm jobs like home building. Many operate small businesses. When tourists visit Lancaster County, they see Amish farmers plowing fields with horse-drawn plows or hauling tobacco with wagons to their barns. Underneath these outward appearances is the most important Old Order value: the conservative Christianity and its strict application to everyday life. Religion is the axis on which the Old Order world revolves.

At first glance, it looks as if the Plain People are stuck in the nineteenth century, while other Americans race to a new millennium pushed by technological advances like the internet. But, the Old Orders do change—though very slowly. Once totally forbidden anywhere except in a shed along the road, telephones are now occasionally found in Amish shops. The owners need them to conduct business as the Amish move from a largely farming church to a church with an ascending small business community.

"It is stated that nothing ever changes among the Old Order Amish and the Old Order Mennonites," says Hoover. "This is, of course, a myth. Their most conspicuous credo, however, is to view their forefathers and elders with profound respect. Thus, when change threatens the Old Orders, they will accept change slow enough to maintain the sanity of the previous generation."

Another leftover value that fits in with the church's conservative Christian world view is *Gelassenheit*. Kraybill believes *Gelassenheit* is the cornerstone of Old Order values. Pronounced "Geh-las-en-hite", the German word means submitting or yielding to a higher authority. In Kraybill's words: "*Gelassenheit* entails self-surrender, resignation to God's will, yielding to others, self-denial, contentment, and a quiet spirit. This way of thinking undergirds the Old Order culture. It undergirds values, personality, symbols, rituals, and social patterns. The spirit of *Gelassenheit* expresses itself in obedience, humility, and simplicity."

Most mainstream Americans are competitive: "Who is number one?" In contrast, Old Order people stress cooperation: "How can I help my neighbors?" Generally, everybody in Old Order Lancaster County is equal. The good of the community overrides the good of the individual.

"We are taught it is more blessed to serve and give than to dictate and receive," says farmer and gazebo-maker Samuel Stoltzfus.

In Old Order Lancaster County, *Gelassenheit* rules—but it rules in a gentle way.

Another basic Old Order value is brotherhood. Old Order Lancaster County upholds a brotherhood of believers who voluntarily help each other and take care of the needy and elderly. The Old Orders refuse to accept government subsidies; no Old Order person has ever been on welfare. The Plain People are fully employed, learning a demanding work ethic as youngsters, which is retained into adulthood. The Old Orders take care of their own—Old Order persons rarely go to a retirement or nursing home.

The Old Order Churches practice beliefs such as living a daily life to win the respect of outsiders so that you will not be dependent on anybody. And providing for relatives, especially the immediate family. If anyone does not do that, he has denied the faith and is worse than an unbeliever.

"What a blessing it is to be able to have fellowship with fellow man in a brotherhood, to share our joys and sorrows by attending church services, farm sales, and visiting," says Ervin Zimmerman, an Old Order Mennonite farmer and owner of a small sewing machine business. "Sharing is such a value in our journey through life."

Faith is at the center of Old Order Lancaster County. So is family.

As divorce splits families apart and as parents move for job advancement in mainstream America, old-fashioned family values fade. Dad works a job and a half. Mom works, too. Children get less and less attention from their parents. Television and peers influence behavior, often negatively. So Americans yearn for a return to lost family values, such as honesty, kindness, and respect for others.

Old Order Lancaster County never lost its family values. As an example, the Plain People believe that the mother is the center of the home. Her job is to stay home and raise the children. Rarely, if ever, do married Old Order women with children work outside their homes. Raising the children and managing the home are the most important duties for Old Order mothers. And these are duties they relish. Harriet Scott, who belongs to the Old Order River Brethren Church, puts it this way: "I believe the Bible is God's book of directions for my life and feel very devoted to fulfill the instructions given to me by my Heavenly Father. I take very seriously the verse in Titus 2:5 about women being 'keepers at home.' Having had the privilege to be a stay-at-home mother has given me great fulfillment and joy."

While Old Order women are homemakers, their husbands are the heads of the household, especially in spiritual matters. They lead the family in grace at meals; they lead worship in church. "It is important for a father to be the head of the home, as Christ is the head of the church," says Zimmerman. "It's the father's duty to provide for the family and to admonish the children to obey their mother. In the home, the father and mother must work together. We hope and pray that this can stay the same and that the family setting is not broken down so we can keep our strong community in a troubled world."

The home is a very important part of Old Order family life. Most often, grandparents live in a second home on the farm, called a "grandpa house." Extended families are the rule, not the exception, and members of the extended family live nearby. The Old Order

In Old Order Lancaster County, farm work is hard work, and all available hands pitch in. These Amish men and boys are stacking wheat in the hot August sun to take to the threshing machine. (Photo © Keith Baum)

GIDEON FISHER

In the Old Order settlement of Lancaster County, Gideon Fisher was a patriarch. He was the institutional memory of the Lancaster Amish settlement for the better part of the twentieth century.

He started his adult life as a farmer. Then, he built a successful farm implement business. In his old age, he wrote a book called *Farm Life and Its Changes*. He also loved to write letters, composing many to people from around the United States whom he met while selling cabbages at a roadside stand near Intercourse. As an amateur historian, he loved to write, talk, and meet people.

He began his letters this way: "Dear Friends, Greetings in Love." He ended them this way: "We wish you the Lord's blessing and good health."

Quietly, patiently, and effectively, he interpreted the values and beliefs of his conservative, separatist church to writers, scholars, and anybody who visited his farmhouse. Nobody left Gideon Fisher's home without feeling they made a friend. Gideon Fisher was beloved because of his kind heart and honest character.

A neighbor said of him: "He had no enemies."

Just before he died, he wrote this on why the Amish are called the Old Order: "The Amish still practice traditions started in the old countries. We have the same system to hold our church services as it was when the first immigrants came to America. Our

An Amish horse-and-buggy funeral procession bears the bier of Gideon Fischer to his grave. An historian and friend to all, Fisher was held in high esteem in Lancaster County. (Photo © Jerry Irwin)

baptisms are still the same. Our weddings, funerals, services are still the same."

He died at age 83. Hundreds of people attended his funeral. And fifty horse-and-buggy teams formed the funeral procession that bore his bier to an Amish cemetery, a mile from the farmhouse where he lived since his marriage in 1933.

experiences life in a collective fashion. A typical youngster has seventy-five first cousins living within a few miles of home. Family members are always around, providing a lifelong security blanket.

The faith of the Old Order brought them to a new world seeking religious liberty. Their strong families have helped preserve the faith in face of modern pressures. Faith and family are cornerstone values of Old Order Lancaster County. So is farming.

Lancaster County is the breadbasket of the East Coast. It has 4,700 family farms and a powerhouse agricultural economy. About a third of those farms belong to Old Order families—farming is the heartbeat of Old Order life. More than fifty years ago, social researcher Walter Kollmorgen underscored the seminal role of agriculture in the Plain communities. "The Amish farmer is wedded to the land not only in a deep and long tradition of good agricultural practices but farming has also become one of the tenets of the Amish religion," he wrote in a pioneering study done in the early 1940s.

Although the Plain People are branching out into nonfarm jobs as the number of farms declines and the Old Order population increases, farming remains the backbone of Old Order Lancaster County.

Not just farming, but *family* farming.

David Fisher, the Amish man who was holding services in his home at the beginning of this chapter, owns a sixty-seven-acre, thirty-cow, scenic dairy farm that has productive soil. His cropping program includes hay, corn (all of which is fed to the cows), and tobacco. Fisher, and his wife, Anna Mary, have raised five children on the farm. "Farming has given us a good family life," Fisher says. "Like a fence, the farm has protected us from the outside world. We have our four seasons. In spring, we plow. In summer, it's another job. In fall, we harvest.

"The farm is my good time. It's my playground. My farm is the best place for me and my family to work."

Faith, *Gelassenheit*, brotherhood, family, and family farming are mutually strengthening core values. Two other Old Order practices—traditional schooling and plain dressing—help maintain those core values.

One-room Old Order schools evoke images of yesteryear. Virtually extinct throughout the United

Some times the best basket is a dress bottom. This Beachey Amish girl has picked beans from the family garden. (Photo © Jerry Irwin)

States, one-room schools live on in Lancaster County. Scores of these educational relics stand out along country roads. Quaint and nostalgic to outsiders, the schools are an important ingredient in maintaining the Old Order culture.

Old Order children are taught by an unmarried female teacher from the community. The schools have eight grades. These are no-frills schools that focus on the basics: arithmetic, reading, grammar, spelling, penmanship, and the German language. Religion is taught with a soft-touch through Bible readings and songs that praise God. The schools have one purpose: to help youngsters become part of their church and remain in their community as adults. The schools are

Opposite top: Two Old Order Mennonite girls are pulling young tobacco plants from beds for transplanting to fields as two small boys help out. A nineteenth-century mule barn is in the background. (Photo © Jerry Irwin)

Opposite bottom: Using old-fashioned equipment, an Amish farmer bails hay in southern Lancaster County. The Jackson Sawmill Covered Bridge is in the background. (Photo © Jerry Irwin)

During spring auctions in villages like Gordonville, Old Order youngsters and men play a hardy game called corner ball. The object of the game is for the throwers to hit the men inside the circle. When a strike is made, the man vacates the circle. (Photo © Jerry Irwin)

overseen by parents rather than administrators, which is contrary to most mainstream public schools. The parents set the standards for the education of their children. And those standards stress respect for tradition, Christian values, and group identity.

Simply, the Old Order schools support the values taught in the families and homes.

As Christian role models, teachers uphold basic Plain People values of honesty, thrift, cooperation, and love. A lunch prayer comes to the heart of their values: "Father, bless our school today. Be in all we do and say. Be in every song we sing. Every prayer to thee we bring. Bless this food and grant that we may dwell in paradise with thee."

Stoltzfus, Hoover, the Scotts, and Zimmerman belong to different Old Order churches. But, they share a common bond: clothing. They dress plainly, which is another Old Order value. As Christians, the Plain People believe true followers of Jesus Christ must be recognized not only by conduct and speech, but by dress. Plain clothing is so different from mainstream clothing it's impossible for an Old Order person not to recognize he's different. And that's the point: Plain people understand that the church, not the media nor New York City fashion houses, establishes standards for dress.

However, dress among the Old Order people varies. Some common examples of women's clothing include capes, aprons, prayer coverings, bonnets, and modest ankle-length dresses. For men, some common examples are broad-brimmed black or straw hats, broadfall pants, solid blue shirts, suspenders, suit coats without lapel, no neckties, and black vests.

"Plain dress is not salvation, but if we desire to live a humble life and honor God rather than to bring honor to our ourselves, dress does make a difference," Zimmerman says.

Across America, leftover values are breaking down or gone. In Lancaster County, they flourish among its Plain People, who prosper by respecting and practicing them.

Old Order Lancaster County is about leftover values.

DR. HOLMES MORTON

Each September, a special event takes place in Lancaster County. The grounds of the Leola Produce Auction are turned into a benefit auction to support the lifesaving work of The Clinic for Special Children.

Homemade quilts, craft objects, furniture, tools, food, and home supplies are donated by friends of the clinic. And scores of volunteers show up on auction day to take part in a time of fun and fellowship for a good cause. In one day, the auction raises a third of the clinic's yearly budget.

Along with a small staff, Dr. Holmes Morton and his wife, Caroline, operate the clinic outside of Strasburg. It's a primary pediatric medical service for children with inherited metabolic diseases, serving Old Order Amish and Mennonite families whose children suffer from a high incidence of genetic disorders.

The auction goes to the heart of Lancaster County, bridging its plain and fancy worlds. In the words of Caroline Morton: "It brings together special children, their families and friends to celebrate the joys these children bring to our lives."

In appreciation for Dr. Morton's extraordinary work, the Plain People donated the land for his clinic. And, in the volunteer barn-raising tradition of the Pennsylvania Germans, they "raised" his clinic in the heart of the Amish countryside.

Dr. Morton has received national recognition for his pioneering work on Old Order genetic diseases. A *Reader's Digest* article headline read: "The Doctor Who Conquered a Killer."

In 1997, *Time* magazine produced a special issue featuring fifteen doctors who treat breast cancer, heart repair, failing sight, and other serious illnesses. The issue was dedicated to "a cast of talented innovators employ[ing] new and exciting techniques to become

Dr. Holmes Morton has received national recognition for his work with genetic diseases in Old Order children. He operates the Clinic for Special Children. Here he's treating Jordan Groff, while Jordan's mother, brother, and sister wait for the doctor to finish. (Photo © Keith Baum)

the latest heroes of medicine." Dr. Morton is one of those fifteen doctors. The article about him said Amish traditions may seem archaic to outsiders, but the Amish have much to teach about caring. Nobody knows that better than Dr. Morton.

When he was honored with a humanitarian award from Johns Hopkins University in Maryland, Dr. Morton wrote: "As I care for children with complex and perhaps lethal inherited disorders, I am impressed by the hopes and worth of these children. The Plain People call them God's Special Children.

"They are children who need our help, and if we allow them to, will teach us compassion.

"They are children who need our help, and if we allow them to, will teach us love."

Amish farms are family operations, and everybody chips in. This Amish girl helps in the dairy barn during milking. (Photo © Jerry Irwin)

Plain clothing is a signature of Old Order culture and an expression of the Plain People's Christian beliefs. Men wear broad-rimmed black or straw hats, such as these at an Amish hat shop; black jackets; black pants; and black vests. The look-alike clothes underscore modesty. (Photo © Jerry Irwin)

Top: *The one-room Old Order schools of Lancaster County stress a basic education in eight grades. Virtually all the teachers are single women from the Plain churches. This Mennonite school teacher gives individual attention to a lower-grade pupil. (Photo ©️ Jerry Irwin)*

Bottom: *A sixteen-year-old Amish girl fixes her prayer cap in a mirror. In addition to prayer coverings, Plain women wear capes, aprons, and modest, ankle-length dresses. (Photo ©️ Jerry Irwin)*

⊸ 3 ⊷

THE FARMS
OF LANCASTER COUNTY

FARMER JOHN DAVID Martin is a fortunate man.

Martin lives in the Churchtown area of eastern Lancaster County where he operates a model dairy farm. His seventy-acre farm has sixty cows.

His soil is very fertile. The right conservation practices—such as contour stripping and cover crops—help prevent erosion, protect his water, and reduce his fertilizer bill.

His children represent the sixth generation of the Martin family who have lived on the farm, making the homestead an exceptional example of agricultural stability. Together with his wife, Mary, he has raised three children. Their son, Jonathan, represents the next Martin to take charge of Wheatland Dairy Farm.

A few years ago, Martin placed a conservation easement on the farm, an action that permanently preserves the land. Nobody will ever grow homes on John David Martin's pretty and productive farm.

Main photo: *Lancaster is one of the country's leading dairy counties, with 95,000 cows. Sometimes, cows like to cool off and take a break from their work, as these cows did in a creek below the Jackson Sawmill Covered Bridge. (Photo © Jerry Irwin)*
Inset: *Amos Funk and two helpers grade tomatoes on their farm. These Washington Boro tomatoes are an excellent variety and the first of the season. (Photo © Jerry Irwin)*

"I like working the soil," Martin says. "The Lord gave me the opportunity to farm, and I want to do what I can for Him to preserve the ground and be a good steward."

Mary Martin adds: "The farm provided us with a good opportunity to raise a family. It's a wonderful opportunity to work together. Working together as a family taught our children responsibility and instilled values."

Martin, his family, and his farm typify Lancaster County agriculture. It is seen in Martin's outstanding stewardship to the size of his farm and from the generational stability of the land to the positive attitudes the family has about farm life.

Martin is also fortunate because his farm is located in the breadbasket of the East Coast and in one of the breadbaskets of America. Lancaster County is blessed with productive, prosperous, and elegant farms; an ideal location for marketing products to the East Coast; a farming heritage that dates back to the 1750s; a hardy work ethic rooted in its Pennsylvania German values; an enormous agricultural infrastructure of feed mills, farm equipment manufacturing plants, and hundreds of other farm-related businesses; and very productive soils. Lancaster County is an agricultural powerhouse with a local farming income of more than $800 million a year. Lancaster County's farms create 39,000 jobs and generate about $6.5 billion in related economic activity. Its level of production exceeds that of twelve separate *states*.

"Farming makes Lancaster County a special place," says Tom Daniels, the director of the Lancaster County Agricultural Preserve Board. "Lancaster County is an island of green and an island of sanity in the Boston to Washington, D.C., megalopolis. What sets Lancaster County apart are three things: the land, the people who farm the land, and their conservative attitude rooted in family and community. Most urban dwellers take their food for granted, but in Lancaster County agriculture is part of the community. University of Minnesota professor John Fraser Hart refers to Lancaster County as the seedbed of American agriculture. Agriculture is the engine that drives the Lancaster County economy, draws the tourists, and makes Lancaster County an attractive place to live."

In no way does Daniels overstate the importance of Lancaster County agriculture. From climate to technology and from people to soil, it all comes together in Lancaster County.

Family-owned farms are the heart of Lancaster County agriculture. John David Martin and his wife, Mary, operate a dairy farm in Churchtown. Their son, Jonathan, represents the next generation of Martin farmers. The couple's daughters are Joline (left) and Jacinda. (Photo © Keith Baum)

Lancaster County is a patchwork quilt. Farming is one of its best and brightest patches.

Like the many patches on the quilt, Lancaster County agriculture is diverse in both size and products. It has farmers who make a living raising twenty acres of vegetables and selling them at roadside stands in front of their farm. It also has businesses like Kreider Farms, which grew from a dozen cows and a flock of two hundred chickens into a diverse farming operation with one thousand cows and 1.7 million laying hens. The business supplies farm-fresh products to wholesale and retail markets throughout the Northeast.

"There is no county in the United States that rivals Lancaster County as far as diversity of both crops and animals," says Lloyd Horst, manager of the Leola Produce Auction where farmers sell fruits and vegetables from April to November. The product diversity is remarkable, indeed. Lancaster County farmers grow corn, soybeans, rye, wheat, barley, hay, oats, vegetables, and tobacco. They raise dairy cows, beef cattle, hogs, sheep, and chickens for meat and eggs. Hundreds of food items, ranging from acorn squash to zucchini, are produced on Lancaster County farms. A sampler: applesauce, asparagus, butter, cheese, dill, dried meats, ground beef, horseradish, ice cream, jams, lamb, milk, mushrooms, peaches, pickles, pork ribs, potatoes, pumpkins, rhubarb, smoked ham, sour cream, strawberries, sugar peas, turkeys, turnips, veal, and watermelons. It's not just that they raise such a diversity of crops and animals, it's that they raise them

Lancaster County has thousands of Old Order Amish and Old Order Mennonite farms. This Amish farmer rakes hay on a perfect summer day. (Photo © Keith Baum)

in incredible numbers. Lancaster County has 45 million broilers, 10 million laying hens, 95,000 dairy cows, 250,000 beef cattle, 6,000 sheep, and 335,000 hogs. In total, Lancaster County's farms have more than 55 million animals, more livestock than any other county in the United States.

The production level of the farms is enormously high. Every second, Lancaster County farms produce thirty eggs, six gallons of milk, and one pound of chicken. In a year, the hens lay 2.6 billion eggs, and the cows produce 207,628,000 gallons of milk.

During the peak of the growing season, the Leola Produce Auction will sell 15,000 to 30,000 cantaloupes, 80,000 to 100,000 ears of sweet corn, 3,000 to 7,000 watermelons, and 3,000 to 8,000 pumpkins a day.

Just as a bumper corn crop dwarfs a garden variety corn crop, Lancaster County stands heads above all Pennsylvania counties in virtually every agricultural measure. But the profile of Lancaster County

Lancaster County farms grow bumper crops. And they produce outstanding farmers like Larry Weaver, a cattle farmer from New Holland. Along with his wife, Barb, Weaver is standing in a field of winter barley. (Photo © Keith Baum)

agriculture against a national standard is even more impressive. A report by the U.S. Department of Agriculture Census, which ranks all counties in the United States on a variety of agricultural indicators, underscores why Lancaster County is one of America's most important farming communities. According to the census, Lancaster County is the thirteenth most productive county in the United States. Only twelve irrigated counties in California, Washington, and Florida produce a higher dollar value of farm products than Lancaster County. Lancaster County is the top nonirrigated county in the country. It is also fourth in number of farms, having 4,700, sixth in dairy, third in poultry, fifth in hogs, first in egg production, and first in products sold directly to people at roadside stands and markets.

On the vast landscape of American agriculture, Lancaster County agriculture has one of the highest silos.

Simply, it all comes together in Lancaster County. It starts with the soil. Blessed with the gift of good land, Lancaster County is the Garden Spot of America. The county has fertile soil rarely seen in such concentration. The soils are primarily limestone-based, deep (thirty inches or more to bedrock), well-drained, and capable of supporting maximum crop yields. When adequate conservation measures are used to protect the soils from erosion, these soils, mostly on low, gently sloping valleys, are some of the most productive in the United States. About 60 percent of Lancaster County's soils carry a prime classification—that means they're the best there is.

But such good soil is not without cost—Lancaster County farmland is some of the most expensive in the United States. Developers and farmers compete for land, keeping an upward pressure on prices. In addition, Old Order farmers pay top dollar for farms.

Farms sell for an average of $5,000 per acre. By comparison, the average price for farmland in Pennsylvania is $2,000 an acre. Midwest farmland sells for between $2,000 and $3,000 an acre.

It's not unusual for Lancaster County farmers to

Straw, used for animal bedding, is a common crop on Lancaster County farms. A bale of straw is kicked out to the wagon on the Dwight Hess farm near Maytown. (Photo © Jerry Irwin)

FRESH FOOD AND THANK-YOU-FOR-COMING SERVICE

When it comes to shopping for farm-fresh produce, meats, and cheeses, Lancaster County has little guys and big guys.

The little guys are roadside stands. An example of the big guys is Root's Country Market & Auction in Manheim. First, the little guys.

Roadside farmer stands are a joy of spring, summer, and fall along the country roads of Lancaster County. From spring's first asparagus to fall's last cabbages, the bounty of Lancaster County farms shines at roadside stands.

The family businesses sell oven-fresh breads, jams and jellies, homemade ketchup and root beer, molasses-and-sugar shoofly pies, and chow-chow relish, as well as other kinds of relishes in canned jars. In the fall, they sell pumpkins, Indian corn, squashes, and mums.

Roadside stands are little engines of farm enterprise, pulling the passersby into the heart of Lancaster County: its farm-fresh food. The only thing better than the food is the extra-friendly, thank-you-for-coming service.

Caleb Stauffer has a stand on his eighteen-acre vegetable farm outside of Ephrata called Farmette Gardens. He advertises "Our Own Sweet Potatoes." His customers think he has the sweetest sweet potatoes—not to mention the ripest tomatoes and tastiest apples—in Lancaster County. As he puts it, "They say we have nice, fresh produce."

Stauffer's roadside stand is a delight. But, at the huge Root's market, it would be one of scores of delights.

Seventy-five years ago, Root's Market started out as a poultry auction. Now, it's a smorgasbord of stands selling meats, cheeses, and farm-fresh produce. Also, it features flea-market items like sunglasses, crafts, trinkets, sports caps, and sweatshirts. While Root's has acquired a flea market personality in recent years, it remains at heart a Pennsylvania German farmers' market featuring the good and plenty of Lancaster County farms.

Roadside stands are the little engines of the Lancaster County farm economy. Farms sell homegrown fruits and vegetables at reasonable prices. Customers appreciate the freshness of the products and the extra-friendly service of the roadside stand operators. (Photo © Keith Baum)

Root's Market is vintage Lancaster County Americana, capturing rural flavors and smells: a perfect place to shop-till-you drop, to meet neighbors, and to make new friends.

Though open only on Tuesdays, it attracts 10,000 to 12,000 people each week from central Pennsylvania and neighboring states during the peak of the warm-weather season. Unlike the little roadside stands, the market is huge. It's located on twelve acres, which includes parking. It has 200 to 250 vendors inside and outside of five buildings. And, it has auctions for poultry, produce, and nursery plants.

In Lancaster County, people can shop at the little guys like Farmette Gardens or the big guys like Root's Market & Auction. Wherever they go, they'll get fresh goods and extra-nice service. Lancaster County's roadside stands and farmers' markets serve up good and plenty food in pleasant settings.

pay more than a half million dollars for a farm. For example, in 1996 a 56-acre farm sold for $560,000, or $10,000 an acre. Another 55-acre farm sold for $630,000—just under $11,500 an acre. People are willing to pay big money for good land.

Despite the high cost, the productive Lancaster County soil is at the heart of the region. "The gift of land is the basis for Lancaster County's consistent prosperity and exceptional agrarian culture," says Alan Musselman, a Lancaster land use consultant.

Generation by generation, farm families molded a proud heritage. And the families stayed on the farms. Mom and pop raised their children; then, the children took over. Then, *their* children took over. Many Lancaster County farms of today have been in the same family, often for six to eight generations.

Such agricultural stability is rare in other parts of the country. In Lancaster County, it's commonplace for several reasons. Over the generations, the farm economy has been generally strong. The markets are close by. The supporting agricultural infrastructure of banks, fertilizer companies, and feed mills is large and progressive. Families have maintained a commitment to farming because it provides a good income and a healthy place to raise children.

An important factor in the agricultural stability is the farming heritage. "Lancaster County is great because of our heritage," says Donald Robinson, administrator of the county's Soil Conservation District. "Our people take pride in our farms. They take pride in being farmers. When I came here thirty years ago, I sensed the dignity and pride of being from Lancaster County. The farming heritage is very important. It means a desire to keep children on the farm, the frugality of living to save for farm purchases, and the willingness to pay the high prices for farmland."

Lancaster County agriculture is an American crown jewel because the people who are the stewards of the land understand and uphold the area's heritage. People like Larry Weaver, a cattle farmer from New Holland and operator of Weaverland Valley Farm. A skilled farmer who has earned one of Pennsylvania's top farming honors, the Master Farmer Award, for his management ability and community service, Weaver has never regretted his decision to take over his father's farm. "I loved it right from the beginning," Weaver

says. "Always, I was going to farm. My dad was a good farmer. I wanted to be with him. I was mighty happy when I had the opportunity to start farming. And I've thoroughly enjoyed it. I think the work ethic of this area is second to none. The people are thrifty. Those factors create an area that is well taken care of and well managed. We have pride in our properties. That's why our farms look so good."

Matt Young is another salt-of-the-earth Lancaster County farmer. He's in a partnership with his father, Henry, and brother, David. The Youngs operate Red Knob Farm, a 425-cow dairy in the southern part of Lancaster County. Red Knob Farm is respected for its first-rate management practices and its careful, soil-saving conservation efforts. The Young brothers are like star athletes who do their job so well and who are such consummate professionals that they make it look easy. They're sort of a pair of Joe Montanas on tractors.

"Lancaster County is a great place to farm," Matt Young says. "When I'm feeling discouraged, I say where else can I go to have such productive soil to grow the crops to feed the cows. No place is better than Lancaster County."

Despite the suburbanization Lancaster County is experiencing, its farming heritage and farm economy remain strong. The Youngs are a perfect example of what drives Lancaster County agriculture: pride in their heritage and impressive performance in their fields and barns.

It all comes together in Lancaster County—even the weather, which can be a farmer's chief enemy. Farmers, in general, are always looking up—too much rain, too little rain. In Lancaster County, when they look up, they like what they see. The county has almost a perfect growing climate, with four moderate seasons and forty inches of annual rainfall, which is generally evenly distributed throughout a full growing season. Lancaster County has had dry growing seasons that have hurt yields, but old-time farmers say the county has never experienced a crop failure.

Two-thirds of Lancaster County's 600,000 total acres are farmland. Farms are in every corner of the county. Lancaster County has 4,700 farms, and virtually all of them are family-owned. Those farms average 85 acres compared to the U.S. average of 350 acres. By national standards, Lancaster County farms are pint

Old Order farms account for 1,500, or one-third, of Lancaster County's 4,500 farms. The Old Order farms, like this one near Leola, are known for their well-kept fields and barns. (Photo © Keith Baum)

CELEBRATING THE HARVEST

When September and October roll into Lancaster County, the harvest is at full speed. Tobacco is being cut. The corn is coming down. The growing season, which started in March with the plowing of fields, is closing out.

So it's time to celebrate and have a little fun.

That's exactly what Lancaster County does—with fairs.

Each fair lasts four to five days. Thousands of people show up to take part in contests like the tug-of-war, to watch parades, to talk to friends and neighbors, and, of course, to eat.

Lancaster County has fairs in Elizabethtown, Denver, Lampeter, New Holland, Manheim, Quarryville, Solanco, and Ephrata.

The fairs are a long-standing tradition. In Lampeter, the fair has been held annually for nearly seventy-five years. In New Holland, it's been around for more than sixty-five years. And in Quarryville, there's been a fair for nearly a half century.

The fairs celebrate the good side of Lancaster County—its farms and small towns. A few of them have carnival rides. Others are pure agricultural fairs.

The Solanco Fair is based on agriculture. Farmers

and farm youngsters compete for prizes by showing dairy cattle, hogs, sheep, lambs, and other animals. Also, the fair has exhibitions of fruits, vegetables, canned goods, baked goods, honey, forage, and grains. Many of those exhibits attract women who enjoy sharing the products of their kitchens. The fair also features a tractor-driving contest, a celebrity cow-milking tournament, and a baby parade, where parents dress up their little children in costumes.

But what it has most is mouth-watering food. In the community building, volunteers cook up daily meals of chicken pot pie, beef stew, and ham. The fairgrounds have a dozen food stands. Nobody is on a diet at the Solanco Fair. "If you leave the fair hungry, it's your fault," food committee member Anna Belle Wiley says.

Above: *Lancaster County celebrates the harvest with fairs in its small towns. The Southern Lancaster County Fair stresses the importance of agriculture to the community. This girl is taking part in a hog contest. (Photo © Jerry Irwin)*

sized. How can farmers make a living on such tiny farms?

The farmers farm very intensively; every acre is used. Double cropping—the practice of putting two crops on the same land in one growing season—is common. The farmers plow right up to the road. In addition, Lancaster County has more animals per acre than any other county in the United States. High animal density and intensive cultivation are hallmarks of Lancaster County farms and make it possible for so many smaller farms to prosper.

On a smaller scale than even the pint-sized farms, Lancaster County is overflowing with flower and vegetable gardens. After all, Lancaster County is the Garden Spot of America. Cultivating a kinship with the land has always been a mark of the Pennsylvania Germans. To the farm homemaker, a garden is more than tomatoes and geraniums—it's a source of pride.

Lee Stoltzfus, of Lititz, is an expert on gardens. "The fields, orchards, and gardens of Lancaster County have fed a nation and added color to our lives," he says.

Lancaster County's Old Order Amish women are exceptional gardeners, creatively planting what Stoltzfus calls "roadside ribbon bedding"—their gardens mix flowers into the borders of their vegetable gardens. Why flowers? The answer: "just for pretty." In Stoltzfus's words: "These gardens have plain but dramatic bones. They follow a simple formula of edging rows of vegetables with a ribbon bed of annuals. This bed of brightly colored annuals is meant to dress up the cabbage and sweet corn, and is placed on the side of the garden toward the road."

Another factor that sets Lancaster County apart from most farm counties in the United States is the presence of a sizable number of Old Order farm families.

Top: *Matt and Dave Young operate a progressive 425-cow dairy in southern Lancaster County. The Youngs are outstanding farmers who uphold the area's farming heritage. Matt (left) is shown here with his nephew, David, who works on the Young's farm. (Photo © Jerry Irwin)*

Bottom: *Lloyd and Virginia Weaver welcome spring to their Lancaster County home with a garden of colorful tulips. The garden, which attracts hundreds of visitors, has 20,000 tulips. (Photo © Jerry Irwin)*

A Good Example

Frysville is a country crossroads where Morton Fry presides over Frysville Farms.

It's a remarkable place, and Fry is a remarkable man.

His grandchildren are the ninth generation of Frys who have lived on the farm; the farm has been in the family for more than two hundred years. "The idea of continuity has to be bred into each generation," Fry says. "It's the result of a deep interest in the land and a deep interest in maintaining the family structure."

Morton Fry believes in faith, family, and hard work.

Once Frysville Farms was a dairy farm. Now, it's a lot of little businesses, having greenhouses, dog kennels, and fast-growing hybrid poplar trees. Frysville Farms is a symbol of Lancaster County's rural enterprise—sun-up to sun-down work.

Morton Fry is a symbol of Lancaster County's agriculture stability and its good heart. As he puts it, "We have an overriding concern for our role in society and the example we set not only for our children and

Morton Fry is an enterprising man whose farm has been in his family for more than 200 years. He's watering poinsettias at his greenhouse in Frysville. (Photo © Keith Baum)

grandchildren but for the community as well. We believe in Judeo-Christian values and we try to practice them."

About one-third, or 1,500, of Lancaster County's farms are held in Old Order Amish and Old Order Mennonite hands. In the Old Order communities, farming is as much a way of life as a way to make money. In the Old Order view, farms are social fences that thwart the pressures of modernity threatening the values of their separatist churches.

Whether the farmers work and live by Old Order values or work and live by mainstream values, they are all part of something that adds immeasurable clout to Lancaster County agriculture: its huge agribusiness industry, ranging from small Old Order Amish businesses that make horse-drawn farming equipment to state-of-the art feed mills that use computers and other modern technology. Lancaster County is the nerve center of agribusiness in Pennsylvania and the Northeast. "Lancaster County has the best concentration of agribusinesses anywhere in the country," says John Schwartz, Lancaster County's chief farm extension agent.

Like its agriculture, Lancaster County's agribusinesses are diverse. R.W. Sauder, Inc. is the largest processor and marketer of eggs in the Northeast and the fifth largest in the United States. New Holland North America, Inc. was started in a Lancaster County farm equipment repair shop more than one hundred years ago. Today, it employs 19,000 people in twenty-four countries. It has 5,600 agricultural equipment dealers and 250 construction dealers worldwide. The company's North American headquarters are in Lancaster County. Turkey Hill Dairy makes 12 million gallons of ice cream a year, tenthmost in the nation. Wenger's Feed Mill, Inc. is a modern mill that helps fuel Lancaster County's huge chicken industry. Good's Mill is an old-fashioned mom-and-pop feed mill that serves the little farmers.

It all comes together in Lancaster County and not just agronomically. It comes together in a picture-perfect way—Lancaster County farms are exceptionally pretty.

Gently rolling farmland, lush green cornfields, golden fields of grain, pastures with meandering streams, tidy white farmhouses offset by vegetable and flower gardens, these are the pretty images of Lancaster County agriculture.

"I have seen a lot of farmland in the West and

Lancaster County has strong agribusinesses, like Sauder's Eggs, the largest processor and marketer of eggs in the Northeast. Vera Wike (center) and Barbara Bachtel are candling eggs, or checking them for cracks, at a Sauder plant in Denver, Pennsylvania. (Photo © Keith Baum)

Midwest," says Ronald Bailey, the chief planner on the Lancaster County Planning Commission, a government agency that adopts plans, sets goals, and monitors the progress on matters such as transportation, housing, farmland preservation, and historical preservation. "I have never seen farmland more beautiful than the farms of Lancaster County. In scenic beauty, if not wilderness values, Lancaster County is a place to rival the great scenic wonders of this country, such as Yosemite or Yellowstone."

David Kohl is a professor of agricultural economics at Virginia Tech University. Over his career, he has traveled 3 million miles to give talks on agriculture, conducted 1,500 workshops, and published four books. In his view, Lancaster is a near-perfect farming county. It has the heritage, the agribusiness resources, the extra-fertile soil, the markets, the working landscapes with exceptional pastoral beauty, and the extraordinary farming diversity.

In Kohl's words: "People in Lancaster County realize they've been blessed. And they have a legacy to carry on to the next generation. It all comes together in Lancaster County unlike any other place."

When anything comes together in one place with the force it does in Lancaster County, the synergism produces something extraordinary. In Lancaster County it has produced a family-based agriculture that's an eighth wonder of the world: a beautiful and bountiful breadbasket.

TALKING TURKEY

Gobble, gobble, gobble.

Thanksgiving is one of the year's most traditional holidays. It's especially traditional at the Esbenshade Turkey Farm near Strasburg. Farmer Robert Esbenshade and his wife, Gladys, operate what Esbenshade calls the "oldest turkey farm under the same name in the same place in America."

Esbenshade's great-grandfather, Isaac, started raising turkeys in 1858. And, Esbenshade is the fourth generation to "talk turkey" on the historic, sixty-acre farm.

The Esbenshades raise eleven thousand birds a year. During the Thanksgiving and Christmas holidays, people flock to the farm to pick a fresh turkey for their meal; many return year after year. Once the right turkey is singled out, the Esbenshades do the rest—the bird is a goner. And customers then take their chosen bird home ready for the oven.

The farm has another tradition. For the past twenty years, Gladys Esbenshade has sponsored November tours for elementary school students. About one thousand children take part annually. She shows them slides on turkey raising, lets them look into the

Esbenshade Turkey Farm in Strasburg is the oldest in the country. People have a tradition of buying their holiday turkeys at the farm. Katie Baum is starting the tradition early; at age three, she's ready to chow down. (Photo © Keith Baum)

turkey barn, and conducts a hayride.

"I just enjoy it," she says, referring to both raising turkeys and sharing the farm with the children.

Opposite top: *New Holland North America, Inc., which has its North American headquarters in Lancaster County, is a huge manufacturer of farm machinery. These men are working on a combine. (Photo © Jerry Irwin)*

Opposite bottom: *Good's Mill is an old-fashioned grain operation in northern Lancaster County that serves the small farmers, mostly from the Old Order Mennonite communities. These workers are handling bags of grain. (Photo © Jerry Irwin)*

Overleaf: *Morning fog blankets farms in southern Lancaster County. One of America's leading agricultural counties, Lancaster has 4,500 farms. (Photo © Jerry Irwin)*

4

THE SCENIC LANDS
OF LANCASTER COUNTY

A STREAM TUMBLES through a steep
woodland and waterfalls pour over
giant boulders. On both sides of the
little waterway, great walls of wild,
white rhododendrons stretch along
the banks.

A woman stands on a river over-
look watching a bald eagle rise and then soar on a warm current of air.

A wildflower sanctuary showcases bloodroot, Dutchman's breeches, trout
lily, and trillium. The Bible says Solomon in all his glory was not arrayed like
the lilies of the field.

Thousands of tundra swans drop to rest and refuel in a marshy area as they
head to the arctic reaches of Alaska and Canada, their summer breeding grounds.

All of these places—and many more—compose the natural wonders of
Lancaster County.

The stream is Tucquan Creek, part of the Tucquan Glen/Pyfer Nature

---

Main photo: *Pinnacle Overlook provides panoramic views of the lower Susquehanna River.*
From the precipice, migrating ducks, hawks, tundra swans, and other birds are often seen.
The beautiful spot offers peace and quiet for a young couple. (Photo © Jerry Irwin)
Inset: *The Ferncliffe Wildflower and Wildlife Preserve is a National Natural Landmark.*
The wooden ravine, which is part of the lower Susquehanna River's scenic appeal, has
wildflowers, such as blue phlox (foreground) and Virginia bluebells. (Photo © Jerry Irwin)

Preserve. It flows into the Susquehanna River, which forms the western boundary of Lancaster County.

Bald eagles nest along and fly over the river.

Shenk's Ferry Wildflower Preserve is one of the most beautiful wildflower sanctuaries on the East Coast.

The tundra swans create a spectacular winter scene at the Middle Creek Wildlife Management Area in northern Lancaster County.

Scenic Lancaster County is associated with postcard-pretty farms. Certainly, Lancaster County has the gift of good farmland. But, it has another gift: picturesque natural areas.

The natural areas create an exceptionally pretty patch on the Lancaster County quilt. "Our outstanding natural areas are a surprise in an agrarian community," says Scott Standish, chief of long-range planning for the Lancaster County Planning Commission. "But, they're real treasures. The lower part of the Susquehanna River is like a near wilderness. It has many jewels. They really make Lancaster County a unique blend of farms and natural conservation areas."

Lancaster County's woodlands, wetlands, streams, lakes, glens, serpentine barrens, caves, overlooks, arches, river islands, and especially the Susquehanna River provide habitats for plants and animals, as well as recreational opportunities for county residents. The natural wonders enhance Lancaster County's scenic charm.

The heart of Lancaster County's natural wonders is its southern belt, especially along the lower valley of the Susquehanna River. The Susquehanna River is one of the largest and most important rivers flowing into the Atlantic Ocean. Its drainage basin includes 27,400 square miles in New York, Pennsylvania, and Maryland. And it's the longest nonnavigable river in the eastern United States. The river, which stretches from upstate New York to the Chesapeake Bay, is bordered by steep, wooded hillsides with rich glens. Ducks, snow geese, and tundra swans are often seen. Herons and egrets are common during the summer and fall. Gulls are around through most of the year. "The Susquehanna River is the best natural feature in Lancaster County," says Clyde McMillan-Gamber, a naturalist with the Lancaster County Parks Department.

Tucquan Glen is one of Lancaster County's most spectacular natural areas. Having year-round appeal, the glen slices through steep slopes to the Susquehanna River. In early summer, white rhododendrons bloom. (Photo © Keith Baum)

A majestic river surprise is bald eagles, which in recent years have returned to the lower Susquehanna River. Three nesting pairs have made the river their year-round home. "There is no greater scenic wonder to me than to stand on one of the overlooks to the Susquehanna River and have an eagle rise on a warm current of air or to watch it soar overhead," says Charlotte "Chotty" Sprenkle, the environmental education coordinator of the Lancaster County Conservation District. "The return of the bald eagle to the Susquehanna River is a scenic wonder."

PECO Energy, a Philadelphia-based utility that operates power plants along the Susquehanna River, owns another natural wonder, the Muddy Run Recreation Park, which encompasses 700 acres of beautiful woodland and rolling fields surrounding a 100-acre lake. Whitetail deer abound; small mammals and waterfowl are plentiful. The park's education center contains aquariums with reptiles and amphibians, and for campers, there are 163 sites tucked into the forest.

Tucquan Glen/Pyfer Nature Preserve is one of the most spectacular natural areas in Lancaster County. Some 4,100 acres of the Tucquan Creek watershed are part of Pennsylvania's scenic rivers system; the glen follows Tucquan Creek to the Susquehanna River. A wild and rugged ravine, the glen slices through steep slopes along the river. It has hiking trails that meander

During dry summer weather, the water level of the Susquehanna River drops to expose rock formations called "potholes," which are shaped by the river. The formations surface almost every August near the village of Falmouth in northwestern Lancaster County. (Photo © Keith Baum)

THE PARKS OF LANCASTER COUNTY

Lancaster County is fortunate to have wetlands, nature preserves, lakes, river islands, pristine streams, and bird sanctuaries.

Also, it's fortunate to have an outstanding parks system, a wonderful complement to its scenic lands. The Lancaster County Department of Parks and Recreation maintains 2,000 acres of parkland located in all parts of the county.

Lancaster Central Park, which is located on the southern edge of Lancaster City and in West Lampeter Township, is the flagship of the county's fleet of parks. The park's 544 acres incorporate many attractions and is divided into several distinct sections. The Williamson area has pavilions, barbecue pits, playgrounds, and basketball courts. Nearby Indian Rock provides an excellent panorama of Lancaster City.

The Kiwanis area has mature oak and beech forest along Mill Creek, with several hiking areas. The area has a wooden covered bridge, fields of wildflowers, and two pavilions.

The Kiwanis area also includes a beautifully restored nineteenth-century barn, which is at the center of Lancaster County's environmental education programs. Shuts Environmental Library, which has more than 2,000 volumes, is located in the barn.

The Conestoga area includes the park office, a swimming pool, and three pavilions. Nearby trails provide short and long routes for hikers, bird watchers, or cross-country skiers. In addition, the Conestoga area has the Garden of Five Senses, a collection of raised herb and flower gardens, scent boxes, reflecting pools, and water courses linked by paved walkways.

But Lancaster County's parks system does not begin and end with Lancaster Central Park; many other parks are sprinkled across the county.

Money Rocks County Park offers grand views of farmland, towns, and wooded hills. The park has spectacular outcroppings of rocks, which are patched with lichens, mosses, and ferns.

Chickies Rock Park includes Chickies Creek, Donegal Creek, and several access points to the Susquehanna River. The park's most notable feature is a massive outcropping of quartzite rock towering 200 feet above the river. The vista offers impressive views of York County, Marietta, and farmland in northwestern Lancaster County. The cliffs contain an

Lancaster County has a very good government-operated parks system. Chickies Rock Park, close to the Susquehanna River, is known for the massive outcropping of quartzite rock, known as Chickies Rock, which towers two hundred feet above the river. (Photo © Jerry Irwin)

example of the Acidic Cliff Community, a geologic formation that is associated with vertical exposures of resistant bedrock, ledges, and talus slopes. The park is managed mainly for its natural resources, including wooded areas and grasslands, but remnants of the area's industrial heritage, such as canal walls and iron furnaces, can also be seen.

Stewart Run, a waterway in Pennsylvania's Scenic Rivers System and a part of the Theodore A. Parker III Natural Area, tumbles over rocks and waterfalls to create one of Lancaster County's most pristine streams. Visitors can hike along trails and take in the park's flora and fauna, including violets, trout lilies, ferns, deer, raccoon, and trout.

The 5.5-mile Conewago Recreational Trail, which was once a railroad line, follows the Conewago Creek through farmland and forests. A seventeen-acre day use area, which has a small pond for fishing, is part of the trail. Recreational trails are an important part of the parks system. Lancaster County strives to conserve greenways and abandoned railroad lines suitable for hiking.

When it comes to parks, Lancaster County has it all.

by gigantic rock outcroppings. A variety of wildflowers, ferns, and mosses cover the ground. By Memorial Day, mountain laurels have blossoms. They are white with delicate pink highlights. By the Fourth of July, white rhododendrons are out. Tucquan Glen is also a hemlock forest, and it has dozens of other types of trees, including American basswood.

Simply, Tucquan Glen is wild, wooded, and wonderful.

Many streams flow through southern Lancaster County, and Kelly's Run is a gem. The shallow stream, with its small cascades and large rocks, has sheer vertical rock walls. Ferns and wildflowers sprout along its banks. It has trails for hiking and horseback riding. Sprenkle says this about Kelly's Run: "At the trail head, you think you are just walking through a typical rolling hill landscape of Lancaster County. As you descend the hillside, the air becomes cooler as you reach the stream. The smell of pines and moist, fallen leaves drench the air.

"From the dry open fields and woodlands, you walk into the completely different habitat of the river hills. It is a beautiful walk along a shallow stream that cascades over large boulders in some areas and sheets over large flat rocks to deep, clear pools in others.

"The large rock overhangs provide small areas of shelter for weary hikers and secretive raccoons, fox, or other wild woodland creatures. The sheer vertical rocks evoke a true feeling of being alone in the back country."

The Hauer-Trout Run Nature Preserve is another southern Lancaster County gem. Visitors gain entrance by crossing over an abandoned railroad track or wading in Trout Run. "Once you enter the clearing, you are in probably the most scenic, picturesque, pristine forest in Lancaster County," McMillan-Gamber says.

It has wildflowers, such as ginger, bloodroot, and pink lady slipper. Also, it has a common variety of birds, such as wood thrush, cardinals, juncos, red-tailed hawks, and great horned owls. "However, it is the forest, the towering trees, the giant boulders jutting from the landscape that relate a feeling of wilderness," McMillan-Gamber says.

Another lower Susquehanna River site is the Pinnacle Overlook, which rises 700 feet above the river, providing a wide view of the river valley. From the overlook, you can see scenic Lake Aldred, which resulted from the construction of a hydroelectric dam at Holtwood. The eight-mile-long lake features vast fields of wildflowers along its shores.

Pinnacle Overlook offers great bird watching, too. During September and October, many birds can be seen following the river south to reach their wintering areas. The Pinnacle Overlook offers great views of migrating waterfowl, hawks, and insects. Tundra swans, Canada geese, snow geese, bufflehead, American black ducks, and common mergansers can be seen passing by and in front of the rock face in the late fall and early winter.

Ring-billed gulls, Bonaparte's gulls, forester terns, ospreys, and bald eagles are part of the Pinnacle Overlook landscape. During the peak migration months of September, October, and November, visitors can see red-tailed hawks, broad-winged hawks, sharp-shinned hawks, and migrating monarch butterflies en route to Mexico.

Bird watchers love the Susquehanna River because it's a major resting and feeding area for shore and water birds migrating from the Arctic to the Atlantic Ocean. The Conejohela Flats, the islands and sandbars of the Susquehanna River directly west of the village of Washington Boro, host a variety of shorebirds and waterfowl almost every month of the year. The National Audubon Society has listed the Flats in their nationwide "Important Bird Areas" program. In February and March, it is a major staging area for tundra swans, pintails ducks, and Canada geese. Ring-billed gulls, greater black-backed gulls, and herring gulls spend winter nights there. In the spring and fall, sandpipers and plovers rest on their yearly migration along the coast. From 1972 to 1988, Rookery Island, an island in the Flats, was the second largest rookery in Pennsylvania for cattle egret and black-crowned night heron. These birds used the island to nest and raise their young in large numbers.

Conejohela is the Susquehannock word for "where the hills slope gently to the river." In fact, this is the one site along the lower Susquehanna River that is a break from the sharp rock cliffs and forests that make up the typical complexion of the shoreline.

The Middle Creek Wildlife Management Area, which is in the northern part of Lancaster County, is owned by the Pennsylvania Game Commission. The 5,144-acre wildlife area is an important site for migrating, nesting, and wintering birds. More than 250 species of birds use the refuge, which includes a 400-acre shallow lake. The most impressive waterfowl siting occurs in January and February with the annual arrival of the tundra swans. Thousands upon thousands of these graceful birds land on the water, where they are

Speedwell Forge is one of a handful of lakes in Lancaster County. Located north of Lititz, the lake is popular with canoeists and anglers. Michelle Thomson, of Lititz, and her children Jamie and Ian enjoy the fall foliage. (Photo © Keith Baum)

joined by snow geese and Canada geese. Throughout the rest of the year, Middle Creek is a migration stop for up to twenty-three species of ducks, herons, egrets, bitterns, rails, plovers, and sandpipers.

"The Middle Creek Wildlife Management Area is probably the best waterfowl area in southeastern Pennsylvania," McMillan-Gamber says.

In addition to waterfowl, Middle Creek abounds with many other animal species. Whitetail deer, ring-necked pheasants, red fox, osprey, marsh hawks, wild turkeys, and songbirds all call the management area home.

The Game Commission has divided and developed Middle Creek into four distinct sections. Its mostly wooded southern ridge and the fringe areas of the main waterfowl development are set aside primarily for hunting. Another section is for public recreation. Included in this area are the visitor's center, four picnic spots, a small fishing pond, and a 40-acre fishing area within the 400-acre lake.

Roughly 750 acres have been set aside for wildlife

propagation. In addition, the wildlife area has hiking, horseback riding, and mountain biking trails.

The fourth section includes most of the agricultural land and has been designated a controlled hunting area.

Each year, tens of thousands of people enjoy Middle Creek's peaceful and beautiful setting to fish, take pictures, hike, bird watch, picnic, and just relax. "Another beauty of the Middle Creek Wildlife Management Area is its peaceful and rural quality," says McMillan-Gamber. "This area is truly a pretty piece of the scenic lands patch on the patchwork quilt of Lancaster County."

Lancaster County's scenic lands include several lakes. Speedwell Forge, on the Hammer Creek in the northern part of the county, is a prime fishing spot. Created by the damming of the creek, the lake is known for walleye, bass, and panfish. In fact, it is one of the best bass fishing lakes in southcentral Pennsylvania.

Octoraro Lake, which is located on the border between southern Lancaster County and Chester County, is a 600-acre artificial lake. The water provides

BIRDLAND

The lower Susquehanna River is a bird watcher's paradise.

Since 1973, some 287 species of birds have been identified. The most obvious birds along the river are aquatic and fish-eating species. Herons and egrets feed on the abundant fish, especially in the summer and fall. Thousands of waterfowl pass through the area during spring and summer migrations, many spending the winter concentrated in open water below area power plants.

Along with the Conejohela Flats—one of the most significant shorebird habitats in Pennsylvania, according to the National Audubon Society—the Conowingo Islands are a special part of the lower Susquehanna River. The beauty of the islands is framed with towering sixty-foot cliffs. Hennery Island and Lower Bear Island, a part of the chain, have been home to nesting bald eagles since 1979. The tailrace at Conowingo Dam is another excellent spot to look for bald eagles. Thousands of gulls also congregate at the dam during much of the year, including such rarities as Iceland, Glaucous, and Thayer's. In addition, the islands are home to warblers, kingfishers, and pileated woodpeckers.

The Susquehanna River in western Lancaster County is a major resting and feeding area for birds migrating from the Arctic and Atlantic Ocean over the Atlantic Flyway. These snow geese are part of the migration. (Photo © Keith Baum)

No wonder environmental educator Charlotte "Chotty" Sprenkle says of the Conowingo Islands, "These truly are the crown jewels of Lancaster County, and their rugged beauty should be preserved forever."

excellent shoreline or boat fishing for panfish, bass, and walleye. In the winter, it is good for crappies.

Muddy Run Recreation Park, a part of the Muddy Run Pumped Storage Project, boasts a 500-acre lake, which is stocked with brook trout and rainbow trout in the spring and fall. It has a spectacular smallmouth bass fishery in the summer. The recreation lake is one of the best spots for winter ice fishing in the southern part of Lancaster County.

A report prepared by The Nature Conservancy has identified the following natural sites as areas of statewide importance that should be protected to preserve the biological diversity of Lancaster County:

Conowingo Island and several surrounding isles form a group of erosional bedrock islands in the Susquehanna River below Holtwood Dam. The great cliffs, numerous huge potholes, and ancient channels make these islands some of the most spectacular riverine bedrock clusters in the country. The islands have a wide variety of plants and contribute greatly to the scenic quality of the lower Susquehanna River. Of the hundreds of plant species found on the islands, the cliff brake fern is the most spectacular. This fragile plant clings to the vertical rock walls of the islands, depending upon rock crevices and leaf litter for growth.

The New Texas Eastern Serpentine Barren and the **Rock Springs Eastern Serpentine Barren** in southern Lancaster County are two of the best examples of this type of community left in the world. Serpentine barrens are mosaics of woodlands, savannahs, and sparsely vegetated clearings. Several rare plants, such as fame flower and scrub oak, are found only on these barrens; the plants are uniquely suited to survive the extremely harsh growing conditions.

Cocalico Creek Wetland is the largest wetland in Lancaster County. It's the best site in the state for a Pennsylvania-endangered species called the bog turtle. This small brown turtle is recognized by the orange, heart-shaped blotch on each side of its head. The turtles prefer wet meadow habitats and marshes. Cocalico Creek Wetland is the perfect habitat for bog turtles.

NATURE AT ITS GLORIEST

F or lo, the winter is past, the rain is over and gone. The flowers appear on the earth, the time of the singing of the birds has come, and the voice of the turtle dove is heard in our land." — Song of Solomon

When the flowers appear on the earth and the turtle dove's voice is heard in Lancaster County, there's no better place to experience the wonder of spring's renewal than in Shenk's Ferry Glen Wildflower Preserve located in Pequea near the Susquehanna River.

The wooded riverside glen is one of the best places on the East Coast to take in wildflowers. It's wild with wildflowers—trillium, trout lily, Virginia bluebells, wild blue phlox, squirrel corn, Dutchman's breeches, violets, columbine, Solomon's seal, May apples, waterleaf, wild ginger, and many more. Some seventy-three species of wildflowers bloom from mid-March

until the end of May. More than sixty other species bloom during the summer and fall.

On some hillsides, almost every inch is covered with wildflowers. Wonderful wildflowers—nature at its gloriest—cover fifty acres of woodland.

Clyde McMillan-Gamber calls Shenk's Ferry "one of the best wildflower areas in the eastern United States and certainly one of the most natural spots in Lancaster County. Few places come near its diversity in woodland wildflowers."

Above: *Naturalists consider Shenk's Ferry Glen Wildflower Preserve one of the best East Coast locations for wildflowers. Virginia bluebells are showcased on a hillside. (Photo © Keith Baum)*

Most people know Lancaster as the Amish County with scenic farms. But Sprenkle and McMillan-Gamber know and appreciate the nonfarm, scenic side of Lancaster County: its natural wonders.

McMillan-Gamber, who finds therapy in the scenic lands of his home county, says: "We need to recognize these areas for the treasures they are and protect and preserve their beauty."

Sprenkle, who has rejoiced in the return of the American bald eagle to the lower Susquehanna River, has an abiding love for the natural beauty of Lancaster

County, especially its southern belt. She enjoys visiting natural habitats across the United States. But few adventures are better than what she experiences in her home county. In her words: "Bounding over the rocks on the river islands, paddling its swirling waters and throwing in a fishing line, hiking with the dogs along the Octoraro Creek or hunting the hillsides and farm fields for pheasants and other small game is coming home. The true beauty of Lancaster County to me is the variety of wildlife, abundance of scenic landscape, and wealth of natural treasures."

Streams like Fishing Creek abound near the lower Susquehanna River. Spring forsythia are in bloom, and an old mill is in the background. (Photo © Jerry Irwin)

5

THE OLD BUILDINGS, BARNS, AND BRIDGES OF LANCASTER COUNTY

BILL AND MARILYN Ebel operate a bed-and-breakfast in Lancaster County called the Gardens of Eden. The inn, which is also the couple's home, overlooks the Conestoga River with terraced grounds of wildflowers, perennials, woodsy trails, and songbirds. Their home is the property's centerpiece. It's an imposing and wonderfully preserved early Victorian-era house built in 1867 by an iron baron.

Built in 1889, Lancaster Central Market is in downtown Lancaster City. The building was built in the Romanesque Revival style of architecture that makes the market one of Lancaster County's most elegant public facilities. The dark red brick and brownstone building has an asymmetrical composition, massive walls, distinctive towers, repetitive use of arches, and ornament sculptures in both stone and terra cotta.

Main photo: *Lancaster County has many exceptionally well-preserved historic buildings, including grand-looking barns. This brick-end forebay barn, which is north of Lititz, is an example of the area's rich architectural heritage. The cross designs on the side are actually omitted bricks, openings which ventilate the barn. (Photo © Keith Baum)*
Inset: *Marieta is a Susquehanna River town that prides itself on the historic preservation of buildings. The Victorian Gothic Revival–style Farmers First Bank has many appealing architectural features. (Photo © Keith Baum)*

Central Market itself predates the building; it has been on the same site since the 1730s. Central Market is the oldest publicly owned, continuously operated farmers' market in the United States. More than eighty stands sell locally grown or produced fruits, vegetables, flowers, meats, breads, cheeses, desserts, and crafts.

In eastern Lancaster County stands Ressler's Mill, also known as Mascot Roller Mill. The mill was built in 1779 with two stories added in the 1800s. As an example of an early stone gristmill, this building is in excellent condition. Lancaster County was a milling center in the 1700s, having more than sixty mills. Now, Ressler's Mill is a museum honoring Lancaster County's milling past.

Wheatland Mansion, which is the historic mansion of President James Buchanan, is a magnificent example of Federal architecture. It was built in 1828 and has large-scale six-over-six window sashes, bold fanlights over doorways, and plain cornice moldings.

The Ebel's home, Central Market, Ressler's Mill, and Wheatland Mansion underscore the diversity and appeal of Lancaster County's architecture. Lancaster County has an impressive number of eighteenth- and nineteenth-century homes and buildings. Its historic public and private architecture, ranging from grand mansions to quaint covered bridges, is among the choicest in the United States.

Lancaster County has approximately 195 individual properties or historic districts on the National Register of Historic Places. These properties include schools, churches, mills, covered bridges, hotels, tobacco warehouses, breweries, farmers' markets, opera houses, farmsteads, plantations, pretzel bakeries, log houses, and chapels.

Historic districts cover dozens of buildings in towns such as Columbia, Strasburg, Lancaster, Lititz, and Marietta. Some towns publish guides that interpret their history and allow people to take walking tours of historical sites and architecturally important buildings from the colonial and Victorian eras.

Columbia grew up on the banks of the Susquehanna River in western Lancaster County. The riverbanks included an elaborate canal system in the early eighteenth century. Columbia was established as Wright's Ferry in 1726, named after the Quaker family that founded it. It was renamed Columbia in 1778. With its prime location, Columbia became a major

James Buchanan was a Civil War–era president from Lancaster County. Wheatland is his historic Federal-style mansion. Volunteers Dave and Dori Schoch have tea on Wheatland's front lawn. (Photo © Keith Baum)

trade crossroads, and in 1789, it came within two votes of becoming the capital of the United States. Later, Columbia was a railroad center. In the early 1900s, the town thrived as an industrial hub with foundries, silk mills, stove manufacturers, and wagon works.

Today, Columbia is no longer a transportation and industrial leader. But its past produced wealthy people who constructed magnificent homes and buildings. For example, The Gallery Along the Susquehanna is a restored 1804 Federal-style building and the birthplace of sonneteer and artist Lloyd Mifflin.

Another Columbia landmark, Hermansader's Victorian mansion, boasts twenty-one rooms. The Queen Anne–style home was built in 1890. The home is a three-story, three-bay, stone and wood-shingled house, featuring a shingled tower, a cross gable that is half-timbered with three double windows, a bay window on the second story, a veranda with clustered posts, and a pedimented entranceway.

The nearby First National Bank Museum is an 1850s bank restored to its original grandeur, with paying and receiving tellers' cages and a president's room.

In eastern Lancaster County, Strasburg stands out as a town with handsomely preserved old homes. Swiss Mennonites settled in the Strasburg area in the early 1700s. A road that connected Philadelphia with the Susquehanna River passed along what is now the Main Street of Strasburg, and the town grew up along the

The Gardens of Eden Bed & Breakfast Inn is a grand Victorian house built in the late 1860s by an iron baron. This interior room, which is in a restored guest house on the property, provides visitors an abundance of beauty. (Photo © Keith Baum)

road with the first building appearing in the early 1730s.

Attracted to the borough's eighteenth- and nineteenth-century buildings, Robert and Cynthia Baker moved to Strasburg in 1986 from Erie in northwestern Pennsylvania. They wanted an old home to restore, and they found what they were looking for in Strasburg. "It has so many homes that still have their original architecture," Mrs. Baker says. The home they bought was built in 1852 and had served as a millinery shop in the early 1900s. Their house is part of Strasburg's historic district. The district, which stretches for 2.5 miles, is a testimony to Strasburg's successful effort to preserve its architectural heritage. The district is on the National Register of Historic Places.

Strasburg's oldest houses were built "on the street" almost without any setback. But, the homes have deep backyards, which are used for flower and vegetable gardens. What is significant about the historic district is the survival rate of the oldest buildings. Twelve of the twenty-nine oldest brick structures survive. All four of the oldest stone homes are intact. And two dozen log homes are part of the district. The survival rate for pre-1815 homes is about 50 percent.

"I am amazed at the wealth of heritage in Lancaster County," says Ronald Bailey, director of planning for Lancaster County. "There are more eighteenth-century houses in Strasburg than in Colonial Williamsburg. Lancaster County has incredible examples of medieval Germanic, traditional English, Georgian, Federal, and vernacular architecture."

Lancaster County's exceptional architectural diversity includes the following historic buildings:

The Old Zion Reformed Church, which demonstrates the Federal style, features delicate woodwork, six-over-six window sashes, and use of circular and oval forms.
Mary Schantz's eighteenth-century limestone farmhouse is a showpiece of English-Gregorian architecture. The property's 1790 barn is one of the finest stone end barns in Lancaster County. Like hundreds of Lancaster County properties, the stone house, stone barn, and wooden washhouse are listed on the National Register of Historic Places.
The Limestone Bed & Breakfast Inn is a two-story house built in 1786 as a family home. Later, it was a headmaster's residence and a dormitory for the Strasburg Academy. The handsome, maroon-trimmed, gray limestone house has a symmetrical five-bay Gregorian facade, and it is one of the most photographed homes in Lancaster County.

The Fulton Opera House, located in Lancaster City, was built in 1852. The landmark structure has a lush Victorian interior, and its second and third stories reflect a Victorian Italianate design with triple-arched windows. As a significant player in America's theatrical heritage, the Fulton Opera House is the oldest continuously operating theater in the United States.
Historic barns abound in Lancaster County. Bank barns, a tradition of Pennsylvania German farming culture, have two stories with a forebay. A forebay is an overhang on the barn's second level that stretches across the full width of the barn without support. From the forebay, a farmer can drop hay to feed the animals. Bank barns are a distinctive regional type of rural architecture.
Three hundred water-powered gristmills once ground grain to produce flour, meal, and animal feed. More than ninety still stand, though only a few operate as mills—many are homes, offices, or museums. They came in many shapes and sizes and were constructed from a variety of materials, including logs, stone, bricks, and wood.

Located in downtown Lancaster City, Central Market is considered one of Lancaster County's treasures. More than eighty stand holders sell meats, cheeses, fruits, vegetables, breads, pastries, and other products. Here, Sam Kauffman and Verna Souders are at the fruit stand, while Donald Warfel operates Mumma's Hand-Twisted Pretzels and Bakery. (Photo © Keith Baum)

So, why is there so much diversity and variety in Lancaster County architecture? Why have so many historic structures survived? "Lancaster County's historically rich ethnic diversity is central to understanding the county's rich legacy of Colonial, Federal, and later periods of architecture," says historian and New Holland resident Willis Shirk.

Lancaster County is a patchwork quilt. Its patch of historic architecture gives it a sense of permanence and harkens back to a time when structures where built to last. In Lancaster County, many homes and buildings have lasted 200 to 250 years. Not only are they beautiful, but the craftsmanship is superior.

Mennonites from Germany and Switzerland were among Lancaster County's first settlers, arriving in the early to mid-1700s. The settlers built homes, churches, and farm buildings that reflected their German heritage.

The Hans Herr House, a sandstone building that reflects this Germanic design, is the oldest structure in Lancaster County. It was built in 1719 by Mennonite Christian Herr for his aging parents, Hans and Elizabeth. Now a museum, it has been restored to its original simplicity and charm. The house has a high-pitched roof that contains two stories within the roofline and a central chimney.

English Quakers were another early group whose tastes are part of Lancaster County's architectural heritage. Wright's Ferry Mansion in Columbia, built in 1738, is an elite example of an English Quaker house. It has a long, narrow form with an interior depth of only one room. The restored house interprets the life of Susanna Wright, an important early resident of Lancaster County. It contains a superb collection of early eighteenth-century Pennsylvania furniture, in addition to fine examples of early textiles, English

ceramics, and glassware.

In addition to Germanic and Quaker architecture, Lancaster County has ornate Georgian architecture, which also originated in England. These buildings have a symmetrical facade that focuses attention on a central doorway. Built from brick or stone, the buildings are two or three stories high.

Rock Ford is an elite example of Georgian architecture. Built in 1794, the brick mansion has survived in very good shape more than 200 years. Its four spacious floors conform to the same plan—a central hall and four corner rooms. The home once belonged to Edward Hand, a Revolutionary War general; today, it is a museum. Rock Ford is an authentic example of refined country living in the early years of the American republic.

Early Victorian buildings are also part of Lancaster County's architectural landscape. These buildings have prominent central domes and monumental porticoes supported by tall columns. Grubb Mansion in Lancaster City's Musser Park is an example of this architectural style, which was influenced by the styles of ancient Rome and Greece.

The grand and ornate Lancaster County buildings like Grubb Mansion contrast with the plain farmhouses in the Old Order communities. Home—along with religion, family, and farming—is at the center of Old Order life. Old Order farmhouses are big, especially the kitchen, but their design is ordinary, reflecting the modest values of the Plain People. Two things distinguish Old Order farmhouses: large porches used for visiting and a "grandpa" house, which is a smaller dwelling attached to the farmhouse. An elderly couple moves into the "grandpa" house when they retire, while their married son or daughter takes over the farmhouse.

Historian Willis Shirk has a passion for old homes, having restored several of them. He understands the appeal of historic architecture. In his words: "Lancaster County's diverse architecture enhances the area's quality of life. The surviving buildings constructed by people of so many diverse ethnic backgrounds serve as visible icons of Lancaster County's rich history. They create a sense of place. They are as distinctive in their diversity as are the white clapboard houses of New England and the brownstone townhouses of Brooklyn or the honey-colored cottages of Cotswolds. This community's historic architecture is undoubtedly the most visible marker on the patchwork quilt that is Lancaster County."

When it comes to architecture, Lancaster County has it all.

Previous pages: *Lancaster County Amish farmhouses are big, but simple in design. The buildings reflect meticulous upkeep and multigenerational use. (Photo © Jerry Irwin)*

A Lancaster County Architectural Gem

Henry Mellinger was a doctor. When his son, David, married in 1892, Henry built a moderately large Edwardian-style house as a wedding gift. Located in the southern part of Lancaster County near Conestoga, the building is known locally as Mellinger Mansion.

Begun in 1892 and finished two years later, the mansion is now a bed-and-breakfast inn operated by Bob and Barb VanderPlate.

The mansion's most striking feature is the perfectly curved turret attached to the northwest corner. It towers four stories, including the roof peak, and incorporates curved glass in all the windows.

The home has multiple angles to it. It has stained glass in all the windows of the third floor. Also, it has many oval windows in the upper floors. All cornices and trim are done with square edges. The property includes 2.2 acres, a two-story carriage house, a two-story barn, and a two-seater brick outhouse with a window. A wrought iron fence surrounds the home.

The most striking feature of the interior is the vast amount of woodwork. Many types of wood, including chestnut, elm, oak, and cherry, are used throughout the house. Ten-foot ceilings accentuate the beautifully finished wood staircases and window sills.

The home has a formal dining room, eight bedrooms, a living room, a breakfast room, parlor, hallway, foyer, full basement, full attic, and 3.5 baths. All the bedrooms have transoms over the doors, which facilitate air circulation. The interior doors of the foyer are inset with etched glass.

Historian Willis Shirk considers Mellinger Mansion one of Lancaster County's grandest buildings. In his words: "I find Mellinger Mansion most striking for its architectural integrity, with its gabled roof, pointed turret, and delicate accents. It is, in my opinion, unsurpassed for sheer picturesque beauty by any of the numerous other late-Victorian-era fairy castles that dot Lancaster County's landscapes."

Above: *Mellinger Mansion is a Victorian-style bed and breakfast inn located in southern Lancaster County. It has an Edwardian design and twenty-two rooms. (Photo © Jerry Irwin)*

THE COVERED BRIDGES OF LANCASTER COUNTY

Like the Amish horse-and-buggy, wooden covered bridges are closely associated with Lancaster County.

The nineteenth-century covered bridges are charming artifacts. With thirty covered bridges scattered across the county, Lancaster County has more covered bridges than any county in Pennsylvania. In fact, except for Parke County, Indiana, Lancaster County has the largest concentration of covered bridges in the United States.

Many of the bridges, interestingly, were named after mills because the water-powered mills were built along the creeks that the bridges spanned. Lancaster County's covered bridges include Risser's Mill, Nissley's Mill, Hess Mill, and Neff's Mill. The Jackson Saw Mill covered bridge, which spans the Octoraro Creek in the southern part of the county, is one of Lancaster County's most attractive covered bridges. The bridge, built in 1878, is 143-feet long and 15-feet wide.

Lancaster County has a crew of workers who maintain the covered bridges as well as the modern bridges. Bob Navitski, the county's assistant engineer,

supervises the crew. Of the covered bridges, he says, "They've woven their way into the local fabric. Residents who live by the covered bridges take them under their wings. They will call me about any problems they see."

Lancaster County residents are fierce guardians of the covered bridges. Lancaster County once had 120 covered bridges, and residents cherish the remaining transportation relics. When a severely damaged bridge is slated to be razed and replaced with a concrete span, residents fight to have it rebuilt as a wooden bridge. When one is destroyed in a flood or a fire, people feel a loss, as if an old neighbor has passed away.

Above: *Lancaster County has thirty covered bridges. Located in the southern part of the county, the Jackson Mill Bridge has a 143-foot span. It's considered one of the county's most attractive covered bridges. (Photo © Jerry Irwin)*

Opposite top: *Mascot Roller Mill, also called Ressler's Mill, is an example of Lancaster County's early stone gristmills. Today, Mascot Roller Mill is a small museum. (Photo © Jerry Irwin)*
Opposite bottom: *Lancaster City's Fulton Opera House is the oldest continuously operating theater in the country. It has a lush Victorian interior. The Actors Company of Pennsylvania is rehearsing "Bye, Bye, Birdie." (Photo © Keith Baum)*

THE ANTIQUES, AUCTIONS, AND MUSEUMS OF LANCASTER COUNTY

LANCASTER COUNTY HAS a passion for antiques, auctions, and museums. The passion goes back to its eighteenth- and nineteenth-century professional artisans and untrained folk artists, who were largely, though not exclusively, centered in the county's Pennsylvania German culture.

Several ethnic groups settled in early Lancaster County. But the largest was the Pennsylvania Germans. They were farmers who worshiped in the Protestant faith. And they were diverse, skilled artisans, such as potters, gunsmiths, weavers, tinsmiths, stonecutters, and glassmakers. Overall, they produced a utilitarian art that reflected their practicality and love of color. They created a very rich body of folk art and furniture that is appreciated and respected beyond this region.

Main photo: *Auctioneer T. Glenn Horst calls a public sale on a farm of Amos Hoover. Auctions are very popular in Lancaster County, and Horst is one of the county's leading auctioneers. (Photo © Keith Baum)*
Inset: *Renninger's Antique & Collectors Market is a mall-like structure that has helped make Adamstown America's Antiques Alley. The market has just about everything under the collecting sun, including these paper-mâché dolls. (Photo © Jerry Irwin)*

"The genius of the Pennsylvania German folk art is the ability to take a highly utilitarian object and decorate it," says Frederick Weiser, a Pennsylvania minister and expert on fraktur, which is a style of broken and illuminated calligraphy.

Fraktur is an example of the decorative arts of the Pennsylvania Germans. Created by hand, it was a significant form of early American folk art designed for special occasions. Though colorful and decorative, fraktur was practical because it fulfilled the function of preserving birth, baptismal, and other records.

That genius of the Pennsylvania Germans showed up in textiles, earthenware, furniture, quilts, linens, and other artifacts. Many generations ago, it established the foundation that has made Lancaster County America's capital of antiques, auctions, and museums.

ANTIQUES

Ruth Bryson lives in a restored stone farmhouse built in 1841 in southern Lancaster County. Her property has a small barn adjacent to the farmhouse and a white fence.

It's the type of place that artists like to draw and visitors like to admire.

The rooms inside are filled with antiques and art pieces that reflect the Pennsylvania German heritage of Lancaster County. Bryson has blanket chests, redware plates, tall-case clocks, frakturs, seed boxes, Dutch cupboards, and kases, or huge wardrobes. These objects, all in very good condition, were made in the eighteenth and nineteenth centuries by skilled Lancaster County artisans.

Her barn is full of antiques from Pennsylvania, New England, and other East Coast regions. Besides collecting top-of-the-line antiques and furnishing her home with them, Ruth Bryson sells them through her business, Country Lane Antiques.

She buys some of her antiques from private sources. But Ruth Bryson is also an avid auction goer; she attends one a week. She checks the sale notices advertised in the newspaper, figures out what she wants, and goes on a buying spree.

Lancaster County has many passions: farming, cooking, and quilting. But, its biggest passion might be collecting and dealing in antiques and going to auctions. Lancaster County is America's antiques and auctions capital. It all comes together in Lancaster

Fraktur is a Pennsylvania German decorative art. An artist created this birth and baptismal certificate, a common use of fraktur, for Anna Gerber in 1788. (Photo © Keith Baum. Fraktur courtesy of Franklin and Marshall College.)

County like it all comes together with Ruth Bryson.

She collects antiques.

She lives with antiques in her home.

She deals in antiques for a living.

And, she goes to auctions.

She has a passion for antiques and auctions, largely because she was born and raised in Lancaster County. "Antiques are the type of objects I'm comfortable with," she says. "I can't relate to modern furniture. Antiques are part of my heritage. I just love the sturdy Pennsylvania German furniture made by skilled craftsmen. I love going to auctions. If I like something at an auction, I'll step up and buy it."

Lancaster County collects antiques like the government collects taxes—nonstop.

Many people in Lancaster County live with antiques, making them a personal part of their households. Many people in Lancaster County deal in antiques, full-time and part-time.

To call Lancaster County America's antiques capital is no exaggeration. Antiques were always a part of business and social life in Lancaster County. But in the past thirty years—largely through the development of the Adamstown area in the northern part of the county into what is called America's Antiques Alley—Lancaster County has acquired a national, if not international, reputation as the place to deal in antiques. Simply, everything old is for sale in Adamstown.

Elias Beiler has an annual farm equipment sale in late February. The sale has seats and other parts for old tractors. (Photo © Keith Baum)

JOY'S ANTIQUES

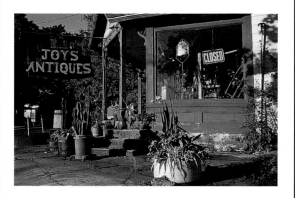

The backcountry roads of Lancaster County have many appealing antiques shops. Joy's Antiques is in an old country store in the village of Little Britain. (Photo © Jerry Irwin)

Lancaster County is an antiques heaven. Some of the best places to hunt for antiques are quaint country shops—like Joy's Antiques.

Joy's Antiques is really off the beaten path in the southern Lancaster County village of Little Britain. It's worth the trip, because looking for antiques in an old-fashioned country shop improves the looking.

Art and Joy Kushlan are the keepers of Joy's Antiques, which they opened in the early 1970s in a former Little Britain general store. Since then, Joy's Antiques has been an excellent source for old dye cabinets, oak case sewing machines, cider presses, vintage clothing, pottery, cherry drop-leaf tables, tin-punched pie safes, church benches, baskets, scales, old postcards, books, wooden wagon wheels, quilts, and especially tools.

People stop in and size up objects. Then, they buy. Country antique shops in old stores are inviting places, and people get hooked.

"We have a little bit of everything," Mrs. Kushlan says. "We like dealing with customers. We enjoy old stuff ourselves. It's fun to sell something when you like it. We try to be reasonable with our prices. And, we try to be friendly."

Stephanie Getz puts a price on an agateware teapot. She sells country store objects such as seed chests, signage, and scales at her stand in Renninger's Antique & Collectors Market. (Photo © Keith Baum)

Lancaster County is mad about auctions. People love to inspect objects at sales before they place a bid. (Photo © Jerry Irwin)

"Lancaster County antiques are characterized by their artistic and structural excellence not found in other areas of the country, like New England," says Bruce Shoemaker of New Providence, an antiques broker and a friend of Ruth Bryson. "Lancaster County furniture was beautifully constructed and built to last. Lancaster County antiques have a charisma and cachet."

Lancaster County is a king-sized version of grandma's attic. Lancastrians hoarded objects and saved things, and antiques were passed down from generation to generation.

By the 1920s and 1930s, the northern part of Lancaster County was a center for antiques shops that wealthy families such as the DuPonts and Rockefellers frequented. The late Hattie Brunner, a longtime Lancaster County dealer, was a grand lady of antiques. She had a sharp eye for objects and a wonderful and gregarious personality that brought national attention to Lancaster County antiques in the 1930s and 1940s. It wasn't until the 1960s, however, that Lancaster County really began to grow into a nationally known,

year-round antiques mecca. At that time, Shupp's Grove on the edge of Adamstown was a place for country and western shows, gospel music, and reunions. An antiques dealer from adjoining Lebanon County organized places to sell antiques, and the tree-lined grove was perfect for the warm-weather months. A nearby farmers' market had vacancies, and the manager offered some antiques dealers indoor spaces for the winter months. The Renninger's Farmers' Market is long gone, but Renninger's Antique and Collectors' Market grew into a huge facility with hundreds of dealers selling all kinds of antiques and collectibles.

In the 1970s, businessman Ed Stoudt opened the Black Angus Antiques and Collectibles Mall, another huge facility with hundreds of dealers, right up the road from Renninger's. Both places have national followings.

Over the years, antiques cooperatives, which are multidealer shops, and stand-alone stores opened up. Adamstown's Antiques Alley is like a shopping mall, with storefront after storefront of antiques stores. Though only open on Sundays, Renninger's and the Black Angus are the anchor stores. The other places,

EVERYTHING, INCLUDING THE KITCHEN SINK

Greetings from Gordonville—home of one of the biggest one-day auctions on the East Coast: the Gordonville Spring Sale.

The sale, which is always held on the second Saturday in March—whether it's snowing, pouring cold rain, or sunny and mild—is sponsored by the Gordonville Fire Company and Ambulance Association. The auction raises funds for the organizations through a small commission on what is sold. And people bring in mountains. Because everything, including the kitchen sink, gets sold, the fire company earns a $40,000 to $50,000 profit.

The Gordonville Spring Sale is a monster event.

In a day's time, forty auctioneers sell new farm equipment, used farm equipment, Amish buggies, horses, mules, new and used hardware, guns, truckloads of hay and straw, and six hundred handmade quilts.

Gordonville is a little town of a couple hundred people surrounded by Amish farms. On sale day, 10,000 people beat a path to Gordonville, where they eat 3,000 sub sandwiches, 4,000 hot dogs, 180 gallons of chicken corn soup, and enough other foods to fill a silo. The sale registers 4,800 bidders.

All the workers are volunteers. The Gordonville Spring Sale merges the plain and fancy world of Lancaster County.

The Gordonville Sale is a huge, one-day March auction that raises funds for the village's fire company. It attracts thousands of mainstream and Amish people. The Amish attend to buy horses, mules, and farm equipment for their spring field work. (Photo © Keith Baum)

Longtime fire company treasurer Ralph Shank oversees the sale; he takes a week off from his job to work at it. "This is a total community effort," Shank says, modestly.

That effort has made the Gordonville Spring Sale an exceptional piece of Lancaster County Americana.

---

mostly open everyday, fill in nicely and offer plenty of variety.

Thousands of dealers, who come from Pennsylvania and other mid-Atlantic states, offer countless objects, such as toys, clocks, model trains, advertising memorabilia, furniture, pottery, vintage clothing, bottles, iron plates, fireplace mantels, books, cans, sheet music, paintings, and much more. If it's an antique or collectible, Adamstown has it.

And, it has it at any price—$8,000 for a grandfather clock, $500 for a quilt, or $10 for a used book.

"Nothing is bigger in the country on a regular basis than Adamstown," Stoudt says. "There's never been an area with such a concentration of antiques markets and dealers." Adamstown has become so big that it has its own trademarked promotional billing: "Antiques Capital U.S.A."

Adamstown takes the marquee billing on the Lancaster County antiques stage. But Lancaster County has hundreds of other antiques shops and antiques

cooperatives in its towns and villages and along country roads. It is likely no county in the United States has more places to shop for antiques. As Lancaster antiques scholar Henry Kauffman wrote: "Lancaster County has been the happy hunting ground for antiques lovers and buyers for many years. There is variety, quantity, and good quality."

These are a few examples of Lancaster County antiques shops:

Fry's Antiques in Strasburg has quality eighteenth- and nineteenth-century furniture.

H. B. Hardican Antiques in Lititz is stocked with nineteenth- and early twentieth-century quilts.

The Ladies Shop in Adamstown has vintage textiles, lamps, upholstered furniture, Victoriana, and vintage decorative arts.

Nailor Antiques in Brickerville features Lancaster County and Shaker decorative arts.

There seems no end to the expansion of the Lancaster

EVERYDAY HISTORY

Henry and George Landis were quite a pair. Bachelor brothers, they were passionate collectors of everyday objects from their childhood until their deaths in the 1950s.

In all, more than 200,000 objects crowded their property north of Lancaster City. They had toys, baskets, butter prints, bookplates, furniture, tools, textiles, clocks, hymnals, bottles, pewter plates, farm implements, and numerous other everyday objects. As factory-made goods replaced handcrafted goods, the brothers resolved they would save objects of the past before they were lost forever.

In 1925, the brothers established a museum on a portion of their property. On their own, and with very little money, they created an amazing portrait of a bygone way of life.

Now, the Pennsylvania Museum and Historical Commission operates the Landis Valley Museum. It's a fascinating living history museum that showcases the rural lifestyle of the Pennsylvania Germans from 1750 to 1900.

Landis Valley Museum is a scenic hamlet with twenty-one structures, including many restored buildings with period furnishings. A log house and outbuildings replicate the building style of Germans who settled Lancaster County in the 1700s. A brick farmhouse shows the lifestyle of Mennonite blacksmith Jacob Landis and his family during the 1830s. The 1870s Landis House is furnished to show how the parents of the museum's founders lived.

Other buildings include shops of a gunsmith,

The state-operated Landis Valley Museum houses an exceptional collection of more than 200,000 Pennsylvania German artifacts in twenty-one buildings. Guides Tom Martin and Susan Kelleher are inside the tavern building with a food spread. (Photo © Keith Baum)

tinsmith, potter, blacksmith, seamstress, and printer. All are equipped with antique tools. These settings, in addition to a tavern, hotel, and country store, provide a backdrop for demonstrations of traditional crafts and trades from late spring through fall. In addition, there are historical landscapes with animals and heirloom plants.

The museum's scenes, structures, and artifacts make it one of the finest collections of Americana in the United States.

County antiques trade. Each year, new cooperatives are built, or existing ones expanded. Each year, Antiques Alley gets a little bigger with the addition of new businesses. On Main Streets of towns or along country roads, somebody is always opening up a new shop.

"When it comes to antiques, Lancaster County has it all," Shoemaker says.

So it does.

AUCTIONS

Auctions are as common in Lancaster County as restaurants are in Philadelphia. Lots of goods go on the auction block in Lancaster County after a death in a family or to raise money: farms, farm machinery, farm equipment, carriages, sleighs, household goods, antiques, buildings, homes, quilts, horses, food, art—you name it.

Lancaster County also has benefit auctions. People donate goods for these auctions—quilts, new furniture, crafts, toys, hardware—for causes such as a medical clinic that helps sick children or a nonprofit charity that helps communities build themselves back up after a natural disaster. All the funds go to the organization, and the auctions always have a mountain of homemade food. As an example, for more than twenty years, the Manheim Christian Day School has had an annual auction, featuring art, quilts, crafts, gift certificates, furniture, and antiques. The auction nets approximately $60,000 for the school.

Fire companies also hold auctions. In March, a half-dozen fire companies sponsor mud sales. Of course, they don't sell mud. The name comes from muddy March with its leftover winter snow and rains. These are popular, all-day events in which everything from lumber to quilts and horses to furniture goes on the auction block. The sales attract thousands. People place goods on consignment with the fire companies, and the firefighters get a small commission when the goods are sold. Towns that have the mud sales include Strasburg, Gordonville, and Gap.

Lancaster County thrives on on-site auctions, which are sales held at country farmhouses or at homes in town. Often, the owners have moved to a retirement center or died, leaving the family to liquidate the estate. Lancaster County has a half-dozen auction houses. The Conestoga Auction House in Manheim and the Horst Auction Center in Ephrata are two of the best, with large and loyal followings.

T. Glenn Horst, of the Horst Auction Center, is one of Lancaster County's top auctioneers. When he stands behind the auctioneer's podium, Horst doesn't need a microphone. His voice broadcasts loud and clear. "I'm blessed with a great voice that really can project," Horst says. Along with his sons, Tim and Tom, his wife, Claudette, and other family members, the Horsts conduct 250 auctions a year at their auction house, on farms, and at homes. The Horsts have called some of Lancaster County's best country auctions. Having been involved with auctions for some forty-five years, nobody knows the business better than Horst. "There are so many auctions in Lancaster County because its people are frugal," he says. "It comes from the Pennsylvania Germans being thrifty. They kept their things. That's why we have so many antiques in Lancaster County."

Besides being a means to do business, auctions are popular social events. People gather to have fun and fellowship. They make friends and eat food. Auctions bring people together.

Horst has seen how auctions bring people together and put them in a good mood.

"A lot of social life revolves around auctions," Horst says. "This is especially true with the Old Order people. When I have a sale at an Old Order farmhouse, all the relatives will come. They may not buy a thing, but they're there for the social life."

The Horst Auction Center is located near Ephrata. It has auctions every Wednesday night. The place is always filled with antiques dealers who want to get new stock, housewives and retirees who want a bargain, and others. Auctions are for all classes of people. A farmer might be sitting next to a doctor. A brick layer might be having a bowl of chicken corn soup and talking about the prices of early-twentieth-century glassware with a lawyer eating a hot dog.

"At our Wednesday night auctions, young people make friends with old people," Horst says. "They go out to eat together. They sit next to each other. It's a good atmosphere."

Besides being fun events, auctions offer the element of surprise. Something special just might pop up between two ordinary pieces of furniture. That's what excites many auctiongoers. As Horst puts it, "It's the find. The thing they're looking for is what nobody else has."

In Lancaster County, the auction business is highly competitive simply because auctions are so popular. No auctions are held on Sunday, but people can go to auctions, which are advertised in newspapers and

Above: *The state-operated Railroad Museum of Pennsylvania is in Strasburg, an eastern Lancaster County community that bills itself as Traintown U.S.A. because of several railroading attractions. The museum has twenty-five locomotives and railcars. (Photo © Jerry Irwin)*

Right: *The Heritage Center Museum of Lancaster County is located in downtown Lancaster City. Its collection features tall-case clocks, furniture, textiles, paintings, and other objects. (Photo © Keith Baum)*

antiques trade publications, every other day of the week.

Few things better capture the flavor of rural Lancaster County than a Horst auction at a farm on a warm, sunny October afternoon. The good weather swells the crowd, a mix of Old Order and mainstream people. Objects come on the auction block at a fast clip. The bidding is strong—everything sells. When a piece of furniture brings an especially high price, people applaud the winning bidder as if to say, "good show." While the auction is going on, some people form small groups to talk and catch up on their neighbor's lives. A fire company ladies' auxiliary sells food and beverages from its lunch truck.

Auctions are an important part of life in Lancaster County. As Horst puts it, "I'm a country auctioneer. We run an honest business, and my children are following in my footsteps. I believe in Lancaster County."

Like Lancaster County believes in auctions.

MUSEUMS

In addition to being a happy hunting ground for antiques lovers, Lancaster County is also a happy hunting ground for museum lovers. "Lancaster County lives for its sense of the past," says Peter Seibert, executive director of the Heritage Center Museum of Lancaster County. "With fifty museums in Lancaster County, history is big business."

The museums are the repositories of outstanding artifacts that tell the story of Lancaster County's cultural heritage.

For example, the Heritage Center Museum, which is located in the center of Lancaster City, features examples of decorative arts. These include coverlets, furniture, pewter, Pennsylvania long rifles, tall-case clocks, paintings, toys, and woodenware. The objects are displayed in the center's historic Old City Hall and Masonic Lodge Hall structures, both dating to the 1740s.

Wheatland is an historic mansion that was the home of President James Buchanan. Situated amidst stately trees, the Federal-period building features family furnishings in period rooms. The mansion is located in Lancaster Township in the same area as the Lancaster County Historical Society. The society has exhibits on county history incorporating fine arts, crafts, and documents.

Rock Ford Plantation is the eighteenth-century home of General Edward Hand, who served in the Revolutionary War. Located in Lancaster City, the property houses the Kauffman Museum, which has an extensive collection of domestic handicrafts and decorative art of southeastern Pennsylvania from the eighteenth and early nineteenth centuries. The museum, which is in a reconstructed eighteenth-century barn, features fraktur, pewter, brass, tinware, carvings, firearms, and furniture.

The Lancaster Mennonite Historical Society, east of Lancaster City, is a fine research center and museum. Its archives include manuscript collections relating to church and family history. The Hans Herr House, which the society owns, focuses on early Mennonite history. It includes the stube or stove room, which is the main room of an early Pennsylvania German house, two tool sheds, and a blacksmith's shop.

Many of Lancaster County's towns trace their history back to the 1700s, so it's common for a town's Main Street to have a museum/historical society. There are twenty such museums in Lancaster County. The Strasburg Heritage Society has its headquarters in the Shroy House, a circa 1790s building, which is the only one-and-a-half-story brick house remaining in town. The 1792 Johannes Mueller House is the home of the Historical Foundation of Lititz. The Winter Heritage House Museum in Elizabethtown interprets the lives of Lancaster County's Scots-Irish settlers in the eighteenth and nineteenth centuries.

One of Lancaster County's best small town museums is the Historical Society of the Cocalico Valley, which is in Ephrata. The society marked its fortieth anniversary in 1997. It is headquartered in the Connell Mansion, a twelve-room brick building with a sandstone facade. Rooms are decorated with period furniture and accessories. In addition to operating the museum, the Historical Society of the Cocalico Valley publishes a scholarly journal and newsletter. It also has a library and research center and a program where experts give talks on historical topics.

The small town museums complement the three state-owned museums in Lancaster County. One, the Ephrata Cloister, was an eighteenth-century communal society rooted in religious mysticism. Ten of its original buildings have been restored to recreate this unusual village. The cloister features fraktur, music, documents, furniture, and broadsheets.

The state-owned Landis Valley Museum, north of Lancaster City, has fifteen buildings housing an exceptional collection of Pennsylvania German artifacts. The buildings feature paintings, fraktur, tall-case clocks, and many examples of Pennsylvania German life.

The Railroad Museum of Pennsylvania in Strasburg is the most popular attraction of the twenty-eight historical sites administered by the state's museum commission. More than 150,000 people a year visit the museum, which promotes the legacy of Pennsylvania railroading from the 1820s to modern times. The museum has seventy-five locomotives and rail cars, a passenger train, and a freight train, in addition to displays that exhibit travel and employment in the rail industry.

One of the county's best museums, the Watch & Clock Museum, is in Columbia. The town is also the headquarters of the 38,000-member National Association of Watch and Clock Collectors, Inc.

The museum illustrates the history of timekeeping. It has more than 8,000 objects, covering four centuries of development from early pocket sundials to the latest in moonphase wristwatches. The timepieces are exhibited in galleries by type and period.

When it comes to horology, nothing beats the Watch & Clock Museum. It has German musical clocks, American clocks from 1800 to 1880, European pocket watches, American railroad watches, tower clocks, cuckoo clocks, tall-case clocks, wristwatches, and nineteenth-century French clocks.

The museum has many unusual and exceptional clocks. A favorite is the Monumental Clock, made by Stephen Engle in 1877. Monumental? The clock is eleven-feet high and nine-feet wide. It weighs hundreds of pounds. The clock edifice has forty-eight moving figures, including the twelve apostles. Each figure measures at least ten inches tall. It took twenty years to build. Monumental? Yes. Magnificent? That, too. When the clock toured the eastern United States, it was promoted as the eighth wonder of the world.

The museum reminds us: *Tempus vitam regit.* The translation from Latin: "Time rules life."

Museums enrich Lancaster County life. Local historian Willis Shirk says this about their importance: "Lancaster Countians appreciate their heritage, and that appreciation is reflected in the extraordinary range of museums and historical sites that thrive in the county. No tourist who seriously wishes to learn something of who Lancastrians are, or where they come from, will ever come away from a vacation here without encountering a plethora of answers that reflect the fascinating complexity of the past."

7

THE SMALL TOWNS AND VILLAGES OF LANCASTER COUNTY

THIS IS THE pretty face of Lititz: a bustling downtown filled with delightful specialty shops, an architecturally inspiring church square, an historic pretzel bakery, a tree-lined Main Street with eight-eenth-century buildings, and a spring  antiques show in Lititz Springs Park where the town band entertains.

All over, Lititz has old charm. It's a storybook, all-American town.

This is Martindale, a Lancaster County village: one-room schools, a family-run country store, horse-and-buggies on roads, lush farms on the outskirts, farmers' roadside stands selling summer and fall produce on the honor system, wash-day clothes hung out to dry along the front porch, and old-fashioned spelling bees in the firehouse.

In Martindale, time has almost stopped.

And, these are the images of Marietta: the Susquehanna River by its side, a Christmas season candlelight tour of restored homes, an arts colony, an historic movie theater, and bed-and-breakfast inns.

Main photo: *Lititz is one of Lancaster County's grand small towns. Its historic buildings, museums, well-kept neighborhoods, and other amenities make Lititz a wonderful place to live or visit. (Photo © Keith Baum)*
Inset: *The Annie Fairfax House is an example of historic Marietta homes. The 1832 home has a Flemish brickwork exterior. (Photo © Keith Baum)*

Marietta's old homes freeze its image in another era.

Lancaster County is a patchwork quilt. One of its prettiest patches is its small towns and country villages. Lititz, Martindale, and Marietta are three of the prettiest.

LITITZ

Our visit to the pretty patch of small towns and villages starts in Lititz, a town of 8,300, located north of Lancaster City.

It's a few days before Christmas and one hundred people are in The Gardens behind the Lititz Museum—the home of the Lititz Historical Foundation—for an evening of Christmas carols. The museum is across the street from the tradition-minded Lititz Moravian Church. The church's trombone choir—itself a tradition of hundreds of years—plays "Joy to the World" and "Silent Night."

As a soft snow falls, the carolers hold small, white candles next to their song sheets. Their voices dance in holiday harmony with the trombone choir. The last act is soloist Bill Stauffer proclaiming for all of Lititz to hear: "O Holy Night." Afterward, the cold carolers warm up with homemade cookies and hot apple cider in the church.

"This is the spirit of the community on display," Stauffer says, of the songfest.

So, it is.

Small towns and country villages are a pretty patch on the Lancaster County quilt, and Lititz is the prettiest part of the patch.

Lititz has it all:

Wonderful traditions, such as the Christmas caroling and one of the oldest, continuous Fourth of July celebrations in the nation at Lititz Springs Park. The event features thousands of candles, doubled in intensity by their twinkling reflections in the water beneath them. In 1997, some 35,000 people joined the celebration.

A sense of history epitomized by its first-rate museum and eighteenth-century buildings still in use along tree-lined East Main Street. One of those buildings is the General Sutter Inn, once the home of Johannes Sutter. Gold was discovered on Sutter's California ranch in 1848, touching off America's greatest gold rush.

A vibrant, beautiful downtown with specialty shops that sell herbs, antiques, and crafts.

Well-kept old homes and buildings that make it a model for historic preservation.

Lititz is a lively town that understands its old roots.

"People love Lititz," says Debrah Mosimann, owner of the Swiss Woods Bed & Breakfast Inn. "It's the nicest small town in Lancaster County, and we hear that time and time again from our guests."

Jean Doherty is the archivist at the Moravian Church. She understands the spell of Lititz. In her words: "For the historical-minded person, Lititz has been beautifully preserved."

Located in north-central Lancaster County, Lititz (population 8,300) was founded in 1756. It was settled by Moravians, who formed a "protesting church" in Bohemia sixty years before the Protestant Reformation. Seeking religious liberty, they came to America and made Lititz their home. Today, the Moravian Church Square showcases some of the town's oldest and most handsome buildings, including Linden Hall, which is the oldest girl's boarding school in the country. It opened in 1742.

History lives in Lititz.

It lives in the Sturgis Pretzel Bakery, which is the oldest commercial bakery in the country.

It lives in the Wilbur Chocolate Candy Americana Museum & Store, which contains antique candy-making objects and a candy store where visitors can really satisfy their sweet tooth.

It lives in the 1742 Johannes Mueller House. The building is the home of the Lititz Historical Foundation.

"Lititz is a Williamsburg of the North," says Ed Crowl, vice president of the historical foundation, referring to the rebuilt colonial Virginia town that's a national tourist attraction. "Nothing here is rebuilt. Lititz is a quaint town."

Above: *Main Street in Lititz showcases eighteen-century buildings, the General Sutter Inn, the 1742 Johannes Mueller House (which is the home of the Lititz Historical Foundation), craft shops, and stores. The shoppers are Curt and Julie Snavely of Lititz. (Photo © Keith Baum)*

Opposite: *Lititz has one of the oldest Fourth of July celebrations in the country. The celebration features more than 4,000 flickering candles, intensified by their twinkling reflection in the water below. (Photo © Keith Baum)*

THE MORAVIAN STAR

Moravians founded Lititz, organizing the first church in town in 1749. Moravians respect tradition. One of their best traditions is the Moravian star. To celebrate Christmas, Moravians around the world hang stars in their churches, from their porches, and in their windows. During the holiday season, Lititz glows with bright, white Moravian stars displayed in downtown stores and neighborhood homes.

The first star, made in 1850 in Europe, was red and white. Around the turn of the century, European stars were generally red, white, and/or yellow, though American Moravians preferred white stars, as they do today.

Since 1958, a fifty-eight-inch, 110-point plastic star has hung in the Lititz Moravian Church during the Christmas season. The 110-point star design was developed in the Moravian school handicraft sessions in Niesky, Germany, in the late 1800s. It's been used in the churches of Herrnhut and Konigsfeld.

The star was constructed by church member Barney Braun. Braun wrote the archivist at Herrnhut to obtain information on the star, and he adapted the design to make a star that fit the church's chancel. The Lititz Moravian Church is the only one in America that uses a 110-point star.

James Hughes is a former pastor of the Lititz church. As he wrote: "Moravians rejoice in the coming

Moravians founded Lititz, and the Moravian star is a Lititz Christmas tradition. The porch of the Moravian Congregational Museum frames a lighted Moravian star. The Moravian church and Brother's House are in the background. (Photo © Keith Baum)

of the Savior, whose birth pierced the darkness of earth's sin like a long-waited star. A beloved hymn expresses their affirmation of faith:

"Morning Star, O cheering sight,
Ere thou camst, how dark earth's night. . . ."

Lititz Moravians believe their many-pointed, bright stars strike peace and hope into every heart.

It's as easy to feel the historical sense of Lititz as it is easy to smell the aroma of candy coming from the chocolate factory. Over the years, the town has added fine eating places and specialty shops to its downtown. In fact, Lititz is a model for how small towns can overcome the impact of suburban shopping malls that have sapped the economic and social vitality of downtowns throughout the United States. Within a few blocks are diverse businesses such as The Herb Shop, Lititz Country Store Antiques, The Main Street Peddler, Another Pretty Face Doll Shop, The Jewelry & Clock Works, Glassmyer's Restaurant with its old-fashioned fountain service, The Teddy Bear Emporium, Ltd., and Ye Old Lititz Framery and Gypsy Hill Gallery.

Jean Doherty says this of her town: "In Lititz, you can put a hanging plant on your porch, and it will be there the next day."

Lively and historically lovely, Lititz has it all. Even the plants are safe in Lititz.

MARTINDALE

Lovina Hoover rides her bike five miles one way from a farm where she lives with her parents to a small school in Martindale. She's the teacher.

The two-story brick building is a parochial school run by the Old Order Mennonite Church. Lovina Hoover has twenty students in grades one to eight. She's the only teacher. Miss Hoover wears a prayer covering and a modest floral-print, ankle-length dress, following the dress rules of her conservative Christian church.

The teacher is twenty years old. She serves up lessons in arithmetic, reading, spelling, English grammar, and the German language. She pounds away at the basics, but she is a caring and gentle boss. "Teaching is something I enjoy," Miss Hoover says. "What I like best is seeing my students understand, and the smiles on their faces when they understand something."

Farming and Martindale go hand in hand. This farmer is using an old-style combine to harvest grain. (Photo © Keith Baum)

Her favorite Bible verse, which she keeps on a paper on her desk, is Proverbs 22:6. It pretty much sums up her work: "Train a child in the way he should go and when he is old he will not run from it."

Miss Hoover's school is a page from the past. So is Martindale. A wonderful page from the past.

Hugged by Old Order Mennonite farms, Martindale is a village of a few hundred people in northeastern Lancaster County. It has a general store, a few small businesses, three churches, and a bunch of old homes. Little has changed in Martindale over the past fifty years because the farmers have held onto their land instead of selling it to developers.

Eby's Store is the village's shopping hub and social center. It's a general store, run by Dick Eby, his wife, Jane, and their three grown daughters. Because the Ebys have had the store for thirty-five years, they know everybody. "We're a family business," Eby says. "Our customers know us. We know them. We're concerned about their problems, not just our own."

Martindale is a page from the past for other reasons besides Lovina Hoover's school and Eby's Store.

Martindale is home to many of Lancaster County's Old Order Mennonite families. Their children go to one-room schools that have eight grades. Teacher Lovina Hoover conducts a lesson in front of the classroom. (Photo © Keith Baum)

A PLEASANT VIEW

We like Martindale with its Old Order Mennonite culture and its quieter ways. Off the beaten path of increasingly crowded and bustling Lancaster County, Martindale is a pleasant place with many pleasant views. In fact, Martindale was once called Pleasant View; the village was renamed Martindale in 1884.

In 1994, Keller Sensenig and Irene Witmer produced a book on the village in northeastern Lancaster County titled *A Pleasant View of Martindale*. Their 300-page book, illustrated with black-and-white photographs, has stories and information on schools, churches, cemeteries, buildings, fires, fatal accidents, mills, bridges, and more.

Like most local history books, the Martindale book was a labor of love. Sensenig and Witmer were working separately on a history of Martindale, just collecting information in a neighborly way. When they found out they were both working on a history of the town, they decided to combine their efforts. It took many years to put the book together.

In the book's conclusion, Witmer wrote: "We have tried to gather these facts for your enjoyment. Some things, which would belong to history but were not so pleasant and could hurt, we have purposely left out. What God has forgiven and cast into the sea of

Martindale is a yesteryear village surrounded by mom-and-pop-sized Old Order Mennonite farms that have served as a buffer against development. A horse-and-buggy travels to church along a quiet road. The Martindale school is at left. (Photo © Keith Baum)

forgetfulness, who are we to bring it up? The 'no fishing' sign remains there."

Only in Martindale, a place where time has almost stopped.

One reason is its old-fashioned farming culture. Old Order Mennonite family farms surround the village. These are sixty-acre farms that have been kept in the same families for five or six generations. They're called mom-and-pop farms because of their relatively small size and because "mom and pop" raise their children on the farms to preserve the separatist way of life preached by the Old Order church.

The Old Order farming culture gives off distinctive signals:

A hand-drawn sign in front of a farmhouse reads: Home Made Butter For Sale.

Wearing an ankle-length dress and a prayer bonnet, a Plain woman walks out of Eby's store holding in both arms a bag filled with groceries. Her two small girls are by her side, almost tugging at her dress. She walks over to the horse tie where she had parked her horse-and-buggy. She puts the groceries in the back of the vehicle. Along with the children, she gets into the seat, and off they go back to the farm.

A wagon at the end of Ivan Burkholder's farm lane becomes a self-service roadside stand. His best cantaloupes sell for only seventy-five cents each. His seconds are ten cents each. Put the money in the box and take your pick.

The firehouse, near Eby's Store, is another social hub. We visited one night when hundreds of people were on hand for a spelling bee, some of which was in Pennsylvania German, a language still commonly used in the village. "It's one of the biggest events in town," says Mervin Martin, a fire company leader and the unofficial "mayor of Martindale." The next day, the fire company had an all-you-can-eat, home-cooked breakfast, featuring sausage, bacon, creamed beef, scrapple, eggs, pancakes, potatoes, fruit, juice, coffee, and donuts. The price: a mere $5.

The village is a center for the Old Order Mennonite Church. But, it's also the home to the mainstream Lancaster Conference Martindale Mennonite Church. Sewing is popular among many women in Lancaster County, especially among women of Mennonite heritage. The church has a sewing circle. When we visited, a dozen women were stitching a beautiful sampler quilt for a benefit auction. The auction is for the Lancaster County–based Mennonite Central Committee, which does relief work and economic development to help needy people throughout the world.

All the quilting is volunteer work—done for a good cause and done from the heart. The quilt sold for $1,525.

"We meet not to get credit for ourselves but to do as our Lord instructs us to do," says Betty Zimmerman, who is in charge of the quilting circle. "That is to share with our neighbors who are local and world-wide that are in need. We want to be like the women in Proverbs 31:20: 'She stretcheth out her hand to the poor . . . yea she reacheth forth her hands to the needy.'"

A few years ago, Martindale residents Keller Sensenig and Irene Witmer wrote a history of the town called A Pleasant View of Martindale. They said despite the urbanization Lancaster County has experienced in the past fifty years, Martindale has retained its nineteenth-century obscurity because it's been "mostly untouched by the outside world."

So it has.

MARIETTA

Thirty years ago, Donald and Michele Neal bought an old home in Marietta. They "fixed it up" by adding a bay picture window and aluminum siding. Like many people do with old homes, they made it look modern.

In recent years, the Neals experienced a change of taste. Doing most of the work themselves, they removed all the interior and exterior modernization, restoring the old beauty and character of the 150-year-old home. The original windows and fanlights in the entryway were returned. The house was painted in colonial colors.

"This home is a wonderful example of the Marietta Restoration Associates' restoration philosophy," says Joyce Heiserman, a leader in the organization that has helped give this Susquehanna River town a national reputation in historic preservation.

A few years ago, the Neals' home was on the preservation organization's Christmas Candlelight House Tour, which attracts 2,000 visitors from

Dick and Jane Eby, who run the general store in Martindale, are surrounded by family. From left to right are: daughter, Deb; sister-in-law, Brenda; grandson, Nicky; daughter, Diane; daughter, Nancy; grandson, Ian; Dick Eby; Jane Eby; granddaughter, Jody; and granddaughter, Alycia. (Photo © Keith Baum)

Pennsylvania and neighboring states. It got rave reviews. Says Neal, "We had so many compliments on it. Our effort has been well worth it."

Like the Neals' home, Marietta gets compliments from visitors throughout the East Coast who enjoy its sleepy, yesteryear feel, bed-and-breakfast inns, sizable historic district, restored Federal and Victorian homes, special events like the Christmas Candlelight House Tour, upscale restaurants and taverns, museums, and the Susquehanna River, which is at the town's doorstep.

Colonial Homes magazine did a nine-page, eighteen-picture piece on Marietta, entitling the article "Susquehanna Ferry Stop" because of Marietta's river history. The article began this way: "Few small country towns in America can claim to have preserved as much of a record of their early history as Marietta."

That's a statement that goes to the heart of Marietta, whose civic motto is: "Restore, restore, and restore."

Marietta (2,800 population) is located in western Lancaster County. It has a prosperous past based on its location by the river and the Pennsylvania Railroad. It was once a lumbering and iron-smelting center, but in the first part of the twentieth century, the river industries declined. So did Marietta's image and economy. But, the town's wealth produced hundreds of handsome Federal and Victorian homes. When the town hit hard times, residents couldn't afford to fix them up. But in 1972, a flood damaged parts of Marietta, and after the water receded, the federal and state governments made low-interest loans available, providing the funds needed for renovation. Untouched, the grand homes were ready for restoration.

The Marietta Restoration Associates provided much of the leadership for Marietta's comeback. The group is a nonprofit, membership organization funded by benefit auctions, dues, and the sponsorship of special events.

Today, about half the town is in an historic district. Scores of homes have been restored. Marietta's restoration effort and its renewal have infused the town with a civic pride. Mrs. Heiserman puts it this way: "People just love to fix up these old homes and see good things happen."

And "good things" have happened to Marietta.

The town has developed a reputation, not only for its restored public and private buildings, but for its cultural events.

Marietta has a garden tour; a music box museum; Shank's Tavern, which is the oldest continuously

operating tavern in Lancaster County; a handful of antiques and crafts shops; a theater built in 1908 that features classic films; an organ with more than 3,500 pipes; and walking tours of the historic district.

A town that has a river on its edge and so many attractive, well-kept, and restored eighteenth- and nineteenth-century buildings is a natural attraction for artists. The Susquehanna River with its islands, vegetation, wildlife, and rock formations and the historic buildings with their pleasing architecture and flower gardens also attract artists to Marietta. The town

Marietta is a town with scores of old homes and other buildings preserved through restoration. Bob Shank is the owner of Shank's Tavern, which is the oldest continuously operating tavern in Lancaster County. (Photo © Jerry Irwin)

inspires creativity.

Kristin Kest is a freelance artist, specializing in zoological, entomological, and botanical subjects. She's exceptionally talented; her work has appeared in guides, the *Farmer's Almanac*, and Reader's Digest books. She could live anywhere but she prefers Marietta, enjoying the river, the old buildings, the flower gardens, and the people. "I just feel in love with this town," she says. "I like its style."

Other artists like Marietta's style, too.

Emilie Snyder's studio overlooks the river from the top floor of her 1814 Federal-style home. The town's historic architecture provides an interesting backdrop to her contemporary paintings. A resident of Marietta for more than fifty years, Anna Mary Loucks does watercolor, oils, and acrylic renderings of Susquehanna

A GRAND HOLIDAY HOMES TOUR

Jeffrey and Stacey Hess's log home with the original clapboard siding, gingerbread accents, and wrap-around porch done in Victorian flavor was on the tour.

So was the Union Meeting House, one of two community-owned buildings restored by the Marietta Restoration Associates, a nonprofit group that promotes historic restoration in the Susquehanna River town.

Many Lancaster County towns have Christmas tours where people can buy a ticket from sponsors and walk through the first level of homes. No tour is bigger or better than Marietta's Christmas candlelight tour, held the first Sunday in December and sponsored by the Marietta Restoration Associates. The event attracts up to 2,000 people, including many on bus tours sponsored by the Smithsonian Institution in Washington, D.C. People come from all over southcentral Pennsylvania and several adjoining states.

The tour earns the organization $20,000 a year while enhancing civic pride. "The whole community pulls together over the tour," says Nancy Kulman, president of the restoration organization.

For the past thirty-four years, Marietta residents have opened the doors of their historic homes so visitors can get a glimpse of Christmas past. Some 130

different homes have been featured over the years. Always, the homes are decorated for the holiday. William and Cynthia Angle decorated their home with dried flowers and herbs from their large garden.

In addition to seeing the interiors of some of Lancaster County's finest old homes, visitors take in an events-packed day. A Civil War church service, an antiques show, holiday shopping in the Old Town Hall Museum and stores, a Civil War encampment, musical presentations, a handbell choral group, a Victorian dance ensemble, and a Victorian tea with cookies and crumpets all vie for the attention of tour participants. With the lighting of the Christmas tree and the singing of carols, a wonderful day closes on a merry note.

For people who enjoy historic, restored homes, food, and entertainment, Marietta's Christmas Candlelight Tour is as good as it gets.

Above: Marietta's Christmas Candlelight Tour showcases the town's historic public and private buildings. This is the Noble House Bed and Breakfast Inn, a restored 1810 Federal-style brick home. (Photo © Keith Baum)

River wildlife. And Judith Johnson has a studio in her 180-year-old home. With its nine-foot, floor-to-ceiling windows, flowered deck, and view of her natural garden, her second-floor studio provides an inspirational working place. Her subjects include portraits of historic Marietta homes.

Not only do artists like Marietta's style, but people who live in other communities appreciate the town's style, too. Some like it so much, they move here. Paul Noble, who relocated to Marietta from the New York

City area, has the same feeling. Marietta has eight bed-and-breakfast inns, including the Noble House that Noble operates with his wife, Elissa. It's vintage Marietta, Victorian decorations in a restored Federal-style brick home built in 1810. Before he moved, he visited Marietta for a getaway weekend. In his words, "It was love at first sight."

"Love at first sight." That's an apt description of Marietta—the river town that saved its past.

Opposite top: Marietta's historic character and proximity to the Susquehanna River inspires artists. Emilie Snyder's studio overlooks the river from the top floor of her 1814 Federal-style home. (Photo © Jerry Irwin)
Opposite bottom: The mainstream Mennonite church in Martindale has a quilting circle. These women are finishing up a sampler-style quilt that was later sold at an auction to benefit the Mennonite Central Committee. (Photo © Keith Baum)

8

THE PENNSYLVANIA GERMAN FOODS OF LANCASTER COUNTY

DEE DEE MEYER is a Pennsylvania German cook.

She lives in Lancaster County where she prepares meals for guests in her Manheim-area home. Diners from all over the United States and many foreign countries call for reservations for her tasty homestyle meals. Not only do they eat, but they eat good and plenty.

Good and plenty. That's the best way to describe Lancaster County's Pennsylvania German food. The cooks prepare good food and plenty of it.

Mrs. Meyer fixes meals that showcase the popular Pennsylvania German cuisine. Her meals are Lancaster County good and plenty at its best. They're hearty, tasty, yet simple. They reflect the Pennsylvania German food tradition or what food writer William Woys Weaver calls a "down to earth style of cooking" that is rich and robust.

"I personally prepare all the food from scratch—bread, salad, two meats, potatoes, fresh-from-the-garden vegetables, relishes, pies, and cakes," Mrs. Meyer

---

Main photo: *Pretzels are a Pennsylvania German tradition. A girl (and her cat) are chowing down on a king-sized soft pretzel. (Photo © Jerry Irwin)*
Inset: *Dee Dee Meyer is a Pennsylvania German cook. Along with her daughter, Miriam, she removes a homemade lemon meringue and concord grape pie from an oven in their Manheim home. (Photo © Keith Baum)*

says. "The recipes have been passed down in my family for years."

She serves foods such as chicken pot pie, chow-chow relish, cracker pudding, noodles with butter, pig stomach, pork and sauerkraut, corn relish, potato buns, shoofly pies, stuffed pickled peppers, sweet bologna, chicken corn soup, bread pudding, sweet-and-sour carrots, and mincemeat pies.

Lancaster County is known for its delicious Pennsylvania German food, the tastiest patch of the patchwork quilt of Lancaster County. Pennsylvania German food is to Lancaster County what Cajun food is to New Orleans: a distinctive regional cuisine. When the Heritage Center Museum of Lancaster County conducted a survey on what makes up the essential ingredients of Lancaster County, the respondents zeroed in on agriculture, industry, and the Plain People. But food and food-related items—like farmers' markets—outnumbered all other categories by more than two to one. Lancaster County is the land of food and cooks, the land of good and plenty.

Pennsylvania German food is heavy and starchy; it is not a lean cuisine. Mrs. Meyer calls it "good old meat and potatoes" food. Somebody said, "If God had wanted us to be skinny, He'd never have invented the Pennsylvania Germans." A Pennsylvania German cooking rule is add butter whenever possible.

Pennsylvania German food—touted by food experts as America's greatest peasant fare—abounds in Lancaster County. Staples include soups, pickled vegetables, meats, jams and jellies, stuffing, breads, puddings, pies, cakes, candies, vegetables, and beverages, such as ginger beer, currant wine, mead, egg punch, and mulled cider. There's an emphasis on hams, sausages, and other pork dishes. Thick with dried beans, peas, and vegetables, soups are central to meals. The cooks love to bake, preparing breads, cookies, and pies. Pies are regular fare at meals. So are sweet-and-sour foods—pickles, preserves, and relishes.

Some Pennsylvania German food is seasonal. The Christmas holiday has a Pennsylvania German sweet side: clear toy candy. Clear toy candy is made from three ingredients: water, very pale corn syrup, and refined white sugar. The candy is molded into animals, trains, and other toy-like objects. The fanciful candy is clear but colorful, made in bright red, green, and yellow. Charles Regennas of Lititz is one of the few

Clear toy candy is a sweet treat. These clear toy bicycle lollipops are made from water, very pale corn syrup, and refined white sugar. The mix is heated and poured into metal alloy molds. (Photo © Keith Baum)

clear toy candy makers left in Pennsylvania. He makes nearly a ton a year, hand pouring the liquid mix into molds. Regennas maintains one of the sweetest Pennsylvania German food traditions.

In Lititz, Minnich's Farm Bakery makes pies, breads, and pastries. But its specialty is sweet-tasting Moravian sugar cake, which is a kneaded yeast cake that has mashed potatoes among its ingredients. After the dough is baked for an hour, holes are punched in the cake. Butter and a mixture of brown sugar and cinnamon are poured into the holes. Bakery owner William Cox says the combination of butter, brown sugar, and cinnamon produce an especially sweet and tasty product.

A sampler of other Pennsylvania German foods includes:

Chicken pot pie. This is like a stew. It's made with dough squares cooked in an open pot over seasoned chicken broth and chunks of poultry.

Shoofly pie. This is a pastry with a wet bottom made from molasses and a crumb top made from flour, sugar, and shortening.

Whoopie pie. This consists of two cakelike cookies held together by a fluffy white icing. Chocolate whoopie pies look like fat Oreo cookies.

Chow-chow. This salad is a medley of fresh vegetables marinated in a sweet-and-sour sauce.

Pickled red beet eggs. Hard-boiled eggs, without

Josiah Glick of Rothsville enjoys a whoopie pie. A whoopie pie consists of two cakelike cookies held together by fluffy white icing. (Photo © Keith Baum)

FASNACHT DAY

Fred Elslager loads up a rack of fasnachts at Holy Trinity Catholic Church in Columbia. Fasnacht Day is the day before Lent. A Pennsylvania German tradition holds homemakers must use up all the lard and fat in their homes before Lent starts. So, they make fasnachts, or donuts. (Photo © Keith Baum)

Blessed are the fasnachts for theirs is the Kingdom of Heaven.

At Holy Trinity Catholic Church in Columbia this is certainly true. Fasnachts are blessed because they raise $20,000 annually for the parish treasury.

Fasnacht Day is the day before Lent, which begins forty days of penance and fasting for Christians. A Pennsylvania German tradition holds that families must use up all the lard and fat in their homes before Lent begins. So, they make fasnachts, which are essentially donuts.

People in Lancaster County are very serious about Fasnacht Day. But, the parishioners at Holy Trinity Catholic Church, who started making fasnachts in 1924 as a fundraiser to build the church, are the most serious. They have an annual fasnacht bake-off where more than one hundred volunteers produce 8,000 dozen—that's 96,000 fasnachts—over the two days before Fasnacht Day.

Anita Grab is in charge of the fasnacht bake-off, which she calls a "labor of love." She claims parish unity, pride, and a secret recipe produce "the best fasnachts in the world."

Prices: $3.25 a dozen for the plain variety, and $4.50 a dozen for glazed fasnachts. For the "best fasnachts in the world," that's a steal.

Forget the diet and chow down.

At Martin's pretzel plant in Akron, Mennonite women hand-twist pretzels. They pass the work day singing gospel songs. (Photo © Jerry Irwin)

Pig's Stomach: A Tasty Pennsylvania German Meal

Just get past the name and you're in for a tasty treat.

Pig's stomach—also called Dutch goose—is a delicious, low-cost meal of ground beef and sausage, diced potatoes, onions, salt, and pepper. Those ingredients are placed inside a scraped and salted pig's stomach. The cook shapes this to look like a goose and then bakes it in a moderately heated oven for three hours. It becomes crisp on the outside. The finished brown skin is a chewy favorite.

Dutch goose is mainly a winter meal, as it's a little on the heavy side.

Joanne Hess Siegrist is a Lancaster County writer and collector of old photographs, which she uses to tell stories about her Mennonite ancestry. She makes Dutch goose once a year to celebrate her Swiss-German Mennonite heritage. In addition, she serves hot apple fritters, buttered peas, chow-chow, celery hearts, whole wheat bread, apple butter, shoofly pie, ice cream, and peppermint tea. During the meal, she plays sixteenth-century Anabaptist hymns and shows slides of Switzerland.

Mrs. Siegrist first prepared the meal in 1968 when she cooked for college friends to express her ethnic background. They liked it, which inspired her to feature the meal for special occasions. When her

children were growing up, their school had annual benefit auctions, and for several years, Mrs. Siegrist put a Dutch goose meal at her home on the auction block. "Once a motorcycle team of six adults purchased the meal," Mrs. Siegrist says. "We made new friends as we exchanged stories around our table.

"Once our oldest son and a van of college students were traveling from Virginia to New York City. They stopped in my home for our traditional meal. I made three large pig stomachs, which turned out to be the most beautiful ones we ever saw. The hearty students ate their platters clean.

"Preparing Dutch goose has always been a special time to stop and remember the ways of our ancestors. This meal tradition will continue in our home just for memory sake."

Above: *Dutch goose, or pig's stomach, is a traditional Pennsylvania German meal that features ground beef, diced potatoes, onions, salt, and pepper. Those ingredients are stuffed into a scraped and salted pig's stomach. Joanne Hess Siegrist prepared this Dutch goose meal. (Photo © Keith Baum)*

---

their shells, are added to a pot of red beet juice. The eggs soak up the flavor and rich color.

Scrapple. This is a combination of meat scraps, spices, and corn meal, formed into a loaf.

Schnitz* and *Knepp. *Schnitz* are dried apples; *Knepp* are dumplings. This dish is a combination of those ingredients, plus seasonings. It's usually made with ham and served like a stew.

A fire company all-you-can-eat, family-style fundraising dinner is a very good place to sample the Pennsylvania German way of cooking, serving, and eating food. Case in point: a chicken-and-waffle dinner conducted by the Blue Ball Fire Company one day in mid-November. Though some of the work was done

in advance, fire company volunteers prepared and served one thousand meals within a few hours. People sat thirty at a table. The volunteers brought the food from the kitchen, spread it before the guests, let them chow down, and then cleaned up the table. Then, they did the same routine again. The menu included chicken, waffles, gravy, mashed potatoes, deep-fried sweet potatoes, peas, pepper cabbage, sliced peaches, relishes, cakes, bread, and ice cream.

The volunteers prepare and serve a ton of food at these dinners. They do 1,300 pounds of chicken, 14 bushels of sweet potatoes, 3.5 bushels of pepper cabbage, 600 pounds of white potatoes, 50 gallons of sliced peaches, 250 loaves of bread, and 45 gallons of ice cream.

Dot Weaver is the president of the fire company's ladies' auxiliary, which works with the fire fighters on the dinner. People wait in line for up to two hours to eat, but the wait is worth it. The meal is good and plenty, Lancaster County style. Dot Weaver explains why: "It's the quality way we make the food. Everything is homemade. If the people don't help themselves, they don't know what they're missing."

The fire company dinner is a bargain. Adults pay $8.50, and they can eat all they want. Every item is passed at least twice down the table.

Like the fire company dinners, butcher shops are a Pennsylvania German food tradition; they dot the landscape in small towns and farming communities. One of the best is Groff's Meats, a fourth-generation family butcher shop in Elizabethtown. Started in 1875, the shop is a landmark. It's run by two sisters—Nancy and Virginia Groff—and two brothers—Franklin and John Groff.

The Groffs are known for their mincemeat pies, which are year-end holiday pies made from apples, raisins, kidney suet, and spices. They are also known for their quality meats, including fresh country sausage, old-fashioned sweet bologna, scrapple, country cured hams, smoked ring bologna, and liver pudding. The service is fast and friendly, and the shop is an old-fashioned place in the best sense of the word. "We put all our effort into the business," Nancy Groff says.

Pretzel making is another Pennsylvania German food tradition. Pretzels came to Pennsylvania from Europe with the German settlers. In Pennsylvania German, a pretzel is a *Brezel*. By the early 1800s, the fat and brown twisted pretzel was a popular Lancaster County snack. In 1861, the Sturgis Pretzel Bakery in Lititz became the first commercial pretzel maker in the United States. The Pennsylvania Dutch Country of south-central Pennsylvania is the Pretzel Capital of the United States.

Most businesses produce pretzels with machines. But a few make pretzels the old-fashioned way: hand-twisting them. Those bakers believe a handmade pretzel is like homemade oven-baked bread: fresher and better. Uncle Henry's Handmade Pretzels in Bowmansville and Martin's Pretzels in Akron still make pretzels

Lancaster County fire companies serve up delicious home-cooked suppers, including turkey, ham, chicken pot pie, and pork. This Blue Ball Fire Company supper features chicken and waffles. (Photo © Jerry Irwin)

Esther Sangrey makes some of Lancaster County's best chow-chow. Chow-chow is a medley of fresh vegetables marinated in sweet-and-sour sauce. (Photo © Jerry Irwin)

by hand.

Local people eat pretzels with ice cream and milk, and there's even a recipe for pretzel soup.

Another Pennsylvania German tradition is canning, especially among Old Order Amish women. Canning cellars are common in Amish farmhouses. Old Order women tend gardens that produce bountiful backyard Lancaster County good and plenty food. Farmer and businessman Samuel Stoltzfus wrote in an Amish periodical: "Gardens are producing well—pole beans, carrots, broccoli, Chinese cabbage, potatoes and tomatoes. Ladies gather them by the apronful, can, freeze, dry or tie up onions, all stored to eat this winter. Let's cultivate thoughts of thanks to the good Lord."

Lancaster County is the land of cooks.

And, Esther Sangrey cooks with the best of them, especially when it comes to making chow-chow. For fifteen years, she had a stand in Lancaster's Central Market. Along with her sister, Dorothy Martin, she sold homemade baked goods, jellies, jams, relishes, and pickles. When she left the stand, she began making

those products for standholder Dan Stoltzfus, who has customers shopping especially for Sangrey's chow-chow and black raspberry preserves.

Mrs. Sangrey was raised on a farm, learning to cook from her mother. Chow-chow is her most popular food. Her explanation for that: "I put more of an assortment of vegetables in it. And, it is more sweet than sour."

Since Lancaster County is the land of food and cooks, it's a center for cookbooks. Likely, Lancaster County is the cookbook capital of the United States. Churches, schools, historical societies, and other organizations produce them for raising funds and other purposes. Titles include *The Strasburg Heritage Cookbook, Family Favorites of the Black Rock Retreat Auxiliary Members, Favorite Recipes from Quilters, The Central Market Cookbook, The Best of Mennonite Fellowship Meals, The Mennonite Community Cookbook, Good Earth and Good Cooking,* and *The East Petersburg Community Cookbook.*

Irene Horst writes a weekly column for a shopping newspaper, focusing on cookbooks and people. Over

HISTORICAL SNACKS

Let's twist . . .
. . . at the Sturgis Pretzel House in Lititz. Lititz is a town overflowing with good history. Being the first commercial pretzel bakery in America, the Sturgis Pretzel House is at the center of the overflow.

The place was a bakery as early as 1784. Legend has it that in the late 1850s a tramp wandered through town and exchanged a hard pretzel recipe for a meal from Julius Sturgis. In 1861, Sturgis opened his pretzel bakery. From this Main Street bakery grew today's pretzel industry.

The pretzel bakery has a lot to offer. The original "soft pretzels" are still made by hand and baked in authentic brick hearth ovens that are more than two hundred years old. In the shop's modern ovens, pretzels move along conveyor belts.

The handsome old building is on the National Register of Historic Places. But visitors are likely to notice something else first: the 4.5-foot high and 6-foot wide display pretzel by the front door. *The New York Times*, in a story it did on the pretzel bakery many years ago, called it the most photographed pretzel in the world. People poke their heads through the holes and say "cheese"—as in cheese pretzel.

Tours allow visitors to see the old and modern ovens. Visitors get a piece of dough to twist into a pretzel, earning them an official pretzel twister's

Pretzel baker Gerald Phillips takes a batch of soft pretzels out of one of his red-brick ovens, which date to 1800. The ovens at the Sturgis Pretzel House in Lititz were first used to bake bread. The Sturgis Pretzel House bills itself as America's first commercial pretzel bakery. (Photo © Keith Baum)

certificate.

Clyde and Barbara Tshudy of Lititz own the bakery. "From two to seventy-two, everybody has a lot of fun," Mrs. Tshudy says. "Our place is fun with a different twist."

twenty years, she has written more than one thousand columns. She has a collection of 125 cookbooks and has also compiled a small cookbook, *The Kitchen Scrapbook*, a collection of recipes, food facts, and inspirational pieces. Her favorite cookbook is *The Mennonite Community Cookbook*. "I learned to cook using it," she says.

Her experiences as a writer, cookbook author, and cook give her special insight into this land of food and cooks. We asked her why Lancaster County is America's Cookbook Capital. Her answer: "People are known here as good cooks. We like to pass on recipes."

In Lancaster County, the food is good and plenty. So are the cookbooks.

Belly up to the table, chow down, and pass on those recipes.

9

THE FUTURE
OF LANCASTER COUNTY

THE FARM OF Dwight and Cheryl Hess overlooks Maytown in western Lancaster County. Their farm is vintage Lancaster County, and so is their family.

Hess feeds out 2,200 beef cattle each year. His crops are corn and small grains like barley, and his soil is especially productive. The land is flat. His eighty-six-acre farm is nearly perfect.

A state-of-the-art farmer, Hess uses computers to manage records, track weather, and keep tabs on the markets.

He's the third generation of the Hess family to live on the farm; the Hess family has very deep roots in Lancaster County. The first were Hans and Magdelena Hess, who left Switzerland in search of religious liberty, settling in Lancaster County in 1717.

Dwight Hess has sold the development rights on his farm to the Lancaster County Agricultural Preserve Board, a public agency that pays farmers to

Main photo: *Lancaster County has lush, scenic farms that shine their best in summer. But sometimes winter adds a different scenic touch, as windblown snow piles up on an Amish farm near Intercourse. (Photo © Jerry Irwin)*
Inset: *The Old Threshermen's Reunion, held on the grounds of the Rough and Tumble Engineers Museum in Kinzers, brings thousands of people into Lancaster County each August. A boy on a small tractor leads the grand parade. (Photo © Jerry Irwin)*

permanently preserve farmland. With those and other funds, he bought more land near his farm to expand his operation and to deepen the Hess family roots in agriculture.

Preserving the farm was an important but tough decision, because residential development had pushed almost to his backyard, making it financially tempting to have the farm rezoned from agricultural to residential use. In addition, farming in the shadow of suburbia produces problems. Sometimes, suburban home owners complain about slow tractors on the roads, farm odors, and water runoff from the farms after heavy rains. Yet, Hess decided with a glad heart.

"I see myself as having a very rich heritage living in Lancaster County," he says. "I want to preserve that heritage for future generations. It really tugs at my heart to see a lot of the development taking place in certain parts of Lancaster County.

"I just would have had a hard time seeing this farm turned into roads and homes. This was an opportunity to preserve this home farm and use some of the funds to acquire more land to add to my farming base and to give me a stronger position in agriculture. The only reason I have an opportunity to farm today is that past generations recognized the productivity of this farm and the heritage of this area. They kept it in agriculture. I could have joined forces with the developers and reaped some impressive revenues by building homes. What gives me the right to turn a good productive farm into housing? I feel an obligation to give future generations the same opportunity I have."

Hess believes land is not inherited from our parents, but borrowed from our children.

In the past twenty years, few public matters have touched such a raw nerve in Lancaster County as the growth/preservation issue. Lancaster County is located in the center of the urban East Coast, between Boston and Washington, D.C. In the talk of real estate agents, "location, location, location" is everything in selecting a home or finding a site for a business. Lancaster County has "location, location, location" of the highest order. As a result, it's one of the fastest growing counties in the Northeast. One fact underscores that. In 1950, Lancaster County's population was 234,000. In the year 2000, it's likely to be in the range of 480,000. In fifty years, the population has doubled. That doubling has pressured Lancaster County's land base, especially the farms. In 1950, Lancaster County had 7,950 farms. Now, it has 4,700 farms. The loss: 3,250 farms, or 65 a year.

The Dwight Hess farm near Maytown has been permanently preserved through Lancaster County's farmland preservation program. The county has saved more than 300 farms. (Photo © Jerry Irwin)

In addition to its ideal location for business and industry, Lancaster County is growing because it has a robust and diverse economy based on agriculture, manufacturing, retail trade, and tourism; good schools; an entrepreneurial ethic that creates jobs; and attractive towns and scenic countryside. It's easy to understand why people move to Lancaster County and why homegrown Lancastrians don't leave.

Because it has it all, Lancaster County is a great place to live and work.

And, because it's Boom County U.S.A., the Lancaster County patchwork quilt is fraying, perhaps fraying too much.

The growth, which accelerated in the 1980s and 1990s, has created many sizable conflicts over land use. Until ten years ago, it appeared the growth horse was galloping through the countryside and nothing could lasso it in.

As Hess took a stand against residential development in his backyard, Lancaster County has taken a stand on growth. But the county's position is not antigrowth or anti-economic development. Lancaster County seeks to better manage residential and commercial development, curb the leapfrogging suburbanization of the countryside, and preserve the area's farming economy and heritage. The plan is based on the premise that Lancaster County can accommodate the growth of the next twenty years and, at the same time, maintain the natural, historical, and architectural heritage that gives the county a sense of place.

Government leaders, preservationists, ordinary

Despite increasing development pressure and decreasing farms, the Old Order presence in Lancaster County remains strong—for now. Today, scenes like this horse-and-buggy passing by an Amish school are common in Lancaster County. (Photo © Jerry Irwin)

citizens, and others have agreed on a plan that has received national recognition as a model for growth management and farmland preservation. The plan centers on a variety of largely public initiatives, which are monitored by nonprofit conservation organizations and citizens organizations. The plan includes the following key parts:

A countywide comprehensive plan. Pennsylvania invests land use decisions in the hands of local municipalities—not the county government. Often, the sixty municipalities of Lancaster County work for their own best interests rather than for the common good. In the early 1990s, Lancaster County government leaders developed a comprehensive plan—a long-term vision for the area's future. With citizen support, it established goals that virtually all local municipal government officials accepted. The goals call for channeling growth in appropriate areas, protecting natural resources, preserving community character, providing for a diversity of park land, and providing for the diverse housing needs of all residents. The plan

Farmer Larry Weaver harvests wheat almost in the backyard of homeowners. The increasing closeness of farmers and suburban homeowners heightens the prospects of disputes over farm odors, farm runoff, and other matters. (Photo © Keith Baum)

PRESERVING THE FAMILY FARM

When it comes to preserving Lancaster County's productive and scenic farmland, no family does it better than the Garbers of Elizabethtown.

Henry Garber is the family patriarch. His sons are Herb, Larry, and Gene.

The Garbers have a passion for farming and a passion for farmland preservation, which is a celebrated cause in Lancaster County. Through public and private sector programs, hundreds of farmers have pledged not to develop their land to secure a strong future for the farm economy. Lancaster County has one of the top farmland preservation programs in the United States.

One reason is the exceptional commitment to preservation made by families like the Garbers. Their farms capture the essence of Lancaster County agriculture—productive, fertile soils, and picture-perfect scenery.

The Garbers care about their heritage and put their beliefs into practice. They've preserved eight farms, more than any family in Lancaster County. The

commitment goes beyond the perpetual conservation easements. Gene Garber serves as a member of the Lancaster County Agricultural Preserve Board and the Lancaster Farmland Trust, which involves countless hours of volunteer work. "Lancaster County has a long tradition of farming," he says. "We have some of the best farmland in the United States. Not to have an appreciation for land like this is wrong. We have generations of ancestors to thank for developing our land into a state of high cultivation. It's important we pass on to our children and grandchildren the opportunity to farm."

Above: *The Garber family of Elizabethtown are leaders in helping to preserve farmland. Father, Henry, is on the tractor. His son, Herb, is on the left. Gene Garber is a tireless advocate of farmland preservation. (Photo © Jerry Irwin)*

is a community-backed vision to take Lancaster County into the twenty-first century the right way.

Urban growth boundaries. Relating to land use and growth management, urban growth boundaries are the heart of the comprehensive plan. Municipalities adopt voluntary growth boundaries around towns or developed areas. On one side of the line, which has the infrastructure, such as sewer and water lines, new homes and businesses can be built. On the other side of the line, agriculture can exist without having to cope with many of the conflicts caused by suburban development. Lancaster County has thirteen urban growth boundaries that allow for 35,000 acres to be developed in the next twenty years.

Agricultural zoning. Virtually all of Lancaster County's townships (thirty-nine of fourty-one) have agricultural zoning that restricts residential development generally to one dwelling for every twenty-five acres and protects the farmers' right to farm. Lancaster County has

380,000 acres in farmland, and some 323,000 acres are protected with effective agricultural zoning. That represents 80 percent of the farmland. Agricultural zoning of the high caliber found in Lancaster County is a rarity in the United States, a fact which underscores this community's dedication to farmland preservation.

Conservation easements. Through the publicly funded Agricultural Preserve Board, Lancaster County pays farmers an average of $2,000 an acre to permanently preserve their land by agreeing to give up development rights. The preservation organization tries to buy conservation easements on farms along the urban growth boundary as an extra buffer against development. The Agricultural Preserve Board is the major guardian of farmland. Lancaster Farmland Trust is a nonprofit conservation organization that also preserves farmland. At the end of 1997, the two agencies have saved 300 farms covering 25,000 acres.

Lancaster County ranks third in the nation in the

Residential and business growth is increasing traffic congestion on Lancaster County roads. Tourists clog roads in villages like Intercourse, where a tour bus shadows an Amish buggy. (Photo © Jerry Irwin)

amount of farmland preserved. However, only about 8 percent of the 323,000 acres zoned for agricultural use have been permanently saved.

Regional planning. The Lancaster County Commissioners have encouraged municipalities with words and funds to cooperate on a regional basis in planning for the future. For example, a landlocked borough has three growing townships around it. In the past, the four municipalities would go their separate ways. Now, their government officials talk to each other and work out problems while maintaining jurisdiction over their own territory.

Though Pennsylvania law invests decision-making power into the hands of municipal officials, it does not prevent them from voluntarily working together. In some instances, Lancaster County municipalities have developed general guidelines for comprehensive

regional plans that focus on roads, sewer and water placements, and parks issues. In addition, the municipalities have established regional police departments and developed greenways and parks.

"Lancaster County is a community, one of the few in the nation, which is making firm commitments and substantial investments to protect its principal resource assets," says Alan Musselman, a Lancaster land use consultant. "Lancaster County will certainly continue to grow and change, but in the context of a sustainable community with an exceptional land ethic."

GROWTH VERSUS PRESERVATION

Communities throughout the United States struggle with the issue of growth versus preservation. But it's likely few communities have struggled with it as mightily as Lancaster County. Angry voices have filled

AGRICULTURAL AMBASSADORS

Andy and Joy.

They're cousins and friends. And they're young Pennsylvanians who are first-class agricultural ambassadors.

Andy Young is the son of Matt Young. Joann "Joy" Young is the daughter of David Young. Matt and David, along with their father, Henry, operate Red Knob Farm, a progressive dairy farm in southern Lancaster County.

The youngsters have had an active role in the farm. That's not unusual—most farm youngsters learn how to work. What's unusual is the advanced achievements of the cousins.

When they graduated from high school in 1996, they planned to attend college. Andy was to study agricultural economics; Joy was to study large animal science. But they had to postpone their college career. For a year, beginning in June, 1996, Andy served as president of the Pennsylvania Future Farmers of America Association (FFA), an organization of 8,300 members. Joy was its vice president.

The two top leaders of a major agricultural organization came from the same farm operation. That's a rare, if not unprecedented, event.

They traveled Pennsylvania, giving talks that

promoted the FFA and that motivated others to develop their leadership skills. They had an exciting but hectic year. Still, they found time to return to Red Knob Farm to milk cows and do field chores—their heads were everywhere, but their hearts were at home.

Andy and Joy are the kind of children that make their parents proud. They're the kind of people that make Lancaster County proud, giving its agriculture a bright future.

Andy Young says: "Lancaster County has one of the most vibrant agricultural industries in the state. Lancaster County has twice as many FFA organizations than any other two counties combined. Its agriculture future looks bright."

Above: *Andy and Joy Young are cousins and leading college-aged ambassadors for Lancaster County agriculture. A few years ago, they held the top two leadership positions in the Pennsylvania Future Farmers of America organization. (Photo © Jerry Irwin)*

public meetings. Citizen groups have protested this new residential development and that new shopping center. Certain developments, like an attempt of the giant retailer Wal-Mart, Inc. in the mid-1990s to build five superstores in Lancaster County, still stir up people and inflame their protests. But, with exceptions, the angry voices have softened in recent years.

The growth/preservation debate will continue well into the twenty-first century.

For the past fifty years, Lancaster County's population has increased by an average of 50,000 people a decade. There's no reason to expect the rate of population growth to ease. Lancaster County has a go-go economy that creates jobs—it has one of the lowest unemployment rates in Pennsylvania. People go where the jobs are, and population growth influences everything, keeping the pressure on the land and creating congestion on the roads.

Lancaster County's roads are clogged. Real road relief appears distant, if not hopeless. Ronald Bailey, planning director for the Lancaster County Planning Commission, makes this insightful comment: "I actually think bad roads may be as distinctive a feature of Lancaster County as good farmland."

Lancaster County has been discovered. And, the Lancaster County Gold Rush is on. But, it looks like Lancaster County won't be mined out—thanks to people like Hess and Darvin Boyd.

Hess is optimistic about the future of Lancaster County, about its agriculture and its heritage. Residential development knocked right against his farm, and he took a stand. So did many of his neighbors. Fifteen contiguous farms, totaling 1,300 acres, are preserved outside of Maytown. "I'm optimistic because of the strong agricultural base in Lancaster County; there's going to be a bright future for agriculture for generations to come," he says.

Boyd took a stand, too.

Boyd was raised on a Lancaster County farm. Now, he's an agricultural banker who lends money to expand

Lancaster County has world-class farmland as this aerial view shows in Paradise. Government officials and private sector leaders have developed a plan to protect farmland and other important aspects of the area's heritage well into the twentieth-century. (Photo © Jerry Irwin)

Lancaster County's farm economy. He's the director of the agri-finance department at First Union Bank in Lancaster, which is one of the largest agricultural lenders in the country. Many people have promoted the cause of farmland/heritage, growth/preservation management in Lancaster County. Nobody has done it with the commitment and common sense of Boyd.

He helped get voter approval of a ballot referendum that established Pennsylvania's statewide farmland preservation program in the late 1980s. He has served as president of Lancaster Farmland Trust. He's a member of the Pennsylvania Agricultural Lands Preservation Board.

He understands Lancaster County.

In his words: "Lancaster County is a national treasure. It is our responsibility to be good stewards and to maintain its rich natural resources to enhance the quality of life for future generations. Let it be our legacy to help the national treasure flourish into the twenty-first century. That indeed is a most noble and worthy vision to fulfill."

EPILOGUE

AMOS HOOVER IS a Lancaster County farmer.

Most people know him not because of his job but because of his avocation. He's an historian and collector of Old Order artifacts—bibles, songbooks, and letters. As the keeper of the Muddy Creek Farm Library, he has a very good handle on the meaning and mysteries of Old Order culture.

When we began working on this book, we asked friends to write some thoughts to serve as the basis for interviews and research. Our question: What is Lancaster County about?

It's about successful family farming, remaining Old Order values, small town living, natural wonders, Pennsylvania German food, preservation of land and historic buildings, traditions, and strong industries and businesses.

Hoover wrote: "I asked my wife, Nora, three times why she likes Lancaster County. She invariably says, 'I like Lancaster County because it is my home.' So I say with her it is our home and with the Psalmist 16:6: 'Our lines have fallen in pleasant places; yea, we have a goodly heritage.'"

He answered the question right.

As we traveled around Lancaster County over the last twenty-five years, we talked with farmers, shopkeepers, entrepreneurs, and Old Order people. In different ways, they would all say the same thing: Lancaster County is blessed.

Blessed with good land.

Blessed with an abiding religious heritage.

Blessed with natural beauty.

Blessed with good people.

Its many blessings boil down to one blessing: a goodly heritage.

Can Lancaster County keep its goodly heritage given its ideal East Coast location that encourages growth, given the expansion/entrepreneur side of its personality, given the inevitable economic/social/technological changes that will cross its borders year after year?

In the late 1990s, Hoover's homestead farm is surrounded by homes. Thirty years ago, his neighbors were cows, not people.

Life is tough. Lancaster County has made tough decisions to try to preserve its goodly heritage in the face of powerful development pressures. Will it succeed?

We're not sure.

But, we hope they do.

Hopefully, the psalmist's words of the Old Testament so eloquently spoken will prevail in Lancaster County in the twenty-first century. "Our lines have fallen in pleasant places; yea, we have a goodly heritage."

Above: Lancaster County's community fairs are fun-filled events. But this boy might have had too much fun. He's taking a nap in a toy tractor during the baby parade at the Solanco Fair. (Photo © Jerry Irwin)
Opposite: Lancaster County has an exceptional heritage that centers on its farms. The sun is setting behind an Amish farm in New Holland. (Photo © Jerry Irwin)

Der Prophet Jonas.

Das erst Capitel.

D As wort des HERRN ist geschehe zum Jona dem sun Amithai...

Das iij. Capitel.

BIBLIOGRAPHY

Bowen, Keith. *Among The Amish*. (Philadelphia: Running Press, 1996).

Daniels, Tom and Deborah Bowers. *Holding Our Ground: Protecting America's Farms and Farmland*. (Washington, D.C.: Island Press, 1997).

Ensminger, Robert. *The Pennsylvania Barn: Its Origin, Evolution and Distribution in North America*. (Baltimore: The Johns Hopkins University Press, 1992).

Friesen, Steve. *A Modest Mennonite Home: The Story of the 1719 Hans Herr House*. (Intercourse, Pa.: Good Books, 1990).

Good, Phyllis and Louise Stoltzfus. *Recipes From Central Market*. (Intercourse, Pa.: Good Books, 1996).

Historic Preservation Trust of Lancaster County. *Lancaster County Architecture 1700–1850*. (Lancaster, Pa.: Intelligencer Printing Company, 1992).

Kauffman, Henry. *Henry's Dutch Country Anthology*. (Morgantown, Pa.: Masthof Press, 1995).

———. *Architecture of the Pennsylvania Dutch Country 1700–1900*. (Morgantown, Pa.: Masthof Press, 1992).

Korber, Kathy and Hal. *Pennsylvania Wildlife: A Viewer's Guide*. (Lemoyne, Pa.: Northwoods Publications, 1994).

Kraybill, Donald. *Old Order Amish: Their Enduring Way of Life*. (Baltimore: The Johns Hopkins University Press, 1993).

———. *The Riddle of Amish Culture*. (Baltimore: The Johns Hopkins University Press, 1989).

Luthy, David. *Amish Folk Artist Barbara Ebersol: Her Life, Fraktur and Death Record*. (Lancaster, Pa.: Lancaster Mennonite Historical Society, 1995).

Rineer, A. Hunter. *Churches and Cemeteries of Lancaster County, Pennsylvania: A Complete Guide*. (Lancaster, Pa.: Lancaster County Historical Society, 1993).

Schneider, David. *Foundations in a Fertile Soil: Farming and Farm Buildings in Lancaster County, Pennsylvania*. (Lancaster, Pa.: Historic Preservation Trust of Lancaster County, 1994).

Scott, Stephen. *An Introduction to Old Order and Conservative Mennonite Groups*. (Intercourse, Pa.: Good Books, 1996).

Siegrist, Joanne Hess. *Mennonite Women of Lancaster County*. (Intercourse, Pa.: Good Books, 1996).

Simpson, Bill. *Guide to the Amish Country*, 2nd ed. (Gretna, La.: Pelican Publishing Company, 1995).

Stoltzfus, Louise, and Jan Mast. *Lancaster County Cookbook*. (Intercourse, Pa.: Good Books, 1993).

Stranahan, Susan. *Susquehanna: River of Dreams*. (Baltimore: The Johns Hopkins University Press, 1993).

Weaver, William Woys. *Pennsylvania Dutch Country Cooking*. (New York: Abbeville Press, 1993).

Wood, Jr., Stacy. *Clockmakers and Watchmakers of Lancaster County, Pennsylvania*. (Lancaster, Pa.: Lancaster County Historical Society, 1995).

Zacher, Susan. *The Covered Bridges of Pennsylvania: A Guide*. (Harrisburg, Pa.: Pennsylvania Historical and Museum Commission, 1994).

An antique German bible from Amos Hoover's collection. (Photo © Keith Baum)

APPENDIX

Selected sources for information on Lancaster County

Columbia Historical Preservation Society
19-21 North Second Street
PO Box 578
Columbia, Pa. 17512
(717) 684-0125

Ephrata Cloister
632 West Main Street
Ephrata, Pa. 17522
(717) 733-6600

Exit 21 Tourist Association
South Pointe Antiques
PO Box 457
Adamstown, Pa. 19501
(717) 484-1026
(Antiques shops and other attractions)

Heritage Center Museum of Lancaster County
13 West King Street
Lancaster, Pa. 17603
(717) 299-6440

Lancaster Downtown Investment District Authority
44 North Queen Street
Lancaster, Pa. 17603
(717) 399-7977

Lancaster Chamber of Commerce & Industry
Southern Market Center
100 South Queen Street
Lancaster, Pa. 17603
(717) 397-3531

Lancaster County Agricultural Preserve Board
Lancaster County Courthouse
50 North Duke Street
PO Box 83480
Lancaster, Pa. 17608
(717) 299-8355

Lancaster County Historical Society
230 North President Avenue
Lancaster, Pa. 17603
(717) 392-4633

Lancaster County Planning Commission
Lancaster County Courthouse
50 North Duke Street
Lancaster, Pa. 17601
(717) 299-8333
(Plenty of information on all aspects of Lancaster County life)

Lancaster Mennonite Historical Society
2215 Millstream Road
Lancaster, Pa. 17602
(717) 393-9745

Lititz Historical Foundation and Museum
137-145 East Main Street
Lititz, Pa. 17543
(717) 627-4636

Marietta Restoration Associates
PO Box 3
Marietta, Pa. 17547
(717) 426-4736

Masthof Press
Route 1 Box 20 Mill Road
Morgantown, Pa. 19543
(610) 286-0258
(Book catalog on Amish, Lancaster County, cookbooks, and other subjects)

Mennonite Information Center
2209 Millstream Road
Lancaster, Pa. 17602
(717) 299-0954

Middle Creek Wildlife Management Area
PO Box 110
Kleinfeltersville, Pa. 17039
(717) 733-1512

PECO Energy
Muddy Run Recreation Park
172 Bethesda Church Road West
Holtwood, Pa. 17532
(Susquehanna River and Conowingo Islands)
(717) 284-4325

Pennsylvania Dutch Convention & Visitors Bureau
501 Greenfield Road
Lancaster, Pa. 17601
1-800-723-8824
(Toll-free number is for obtaining computerized information on obtaining a visitor's guide and lodging.)
(717) 299-8901
(This number is for specific information or questions.)

PP&L
Holtwood Land Management Office
9 New Village Road
Holtwood, Pa. 17532
(717) 284-2278
(Susquehanna River and wildflower preserves)

Root's Country Market & Auction
705 Graystone Road
Manheim, Pa. 17545
(717) 898-7811

Strasburg Rail Road Company
P.O. Box 96
Strasburg, Pa. 17579
(717) 687-7522

Susquehanna Heritage and Tourist Information Center
445 Linden St.
Columbia, Pa. 17512
(717) 684-5249

Young Center for the Study of Anabaptist and Pietist Groups
Elizabethtown College
Elizabethtown, Pa. 17022
(717) 361-1470
(General information on Amish and Mennonite groups)

INDEX

ABOUT THE AUTHOR AND PHOTOGRAPHERS

Ed Klimuska has been a reporter in Lancaster County for twenty-five years. He has won many local, state, and national awards for his writing on the Amish, social and economic problems in Lancaster City, farming, and education, among other topics. His freelance work has appeared in several magazines, such as *Farm Journal* and *Income Opportunities* and in the Voyageur Press anthology, *This Old Tractor: A Treasury of Vintage Tractors and Family Farm Memories*. A native of Wilkes-Barre, Pennsylvania, he now makes his home in New Holland.

Keith Baum is a freelance photographer based in Lancaster County and a member of the SEND International mission agency media team. He spent ten years as a staff photographer for the *Lancaster New Era*, and his work has been published widely by the Associated Press and in many magazines, including *National Geographic*. In addition, his images have appeared in calendars published by BrownTrout and the Sierra Club and in the Voyageur Press books *This Old Tractor: A Treasury of Vintage Tractors and Family Farm Memories* and *The Complete Cow*. A twelve-photo exhibition of his work is part of a permanent exhibit at the National Museum of American History of the Smithsonian Institution. Born and raised in Lancaster County, Keith lives in Rothsville with his wife, Carol, and his two children, David and Katie.

Jerry Irwin is a freelance photographer based in Lancaster County. He has published six books, including *Amish Life* and *Barns of America*. His photographs have appeared in many magazines, including *Sports Illustrated*, *National Geographic*, *Country Journal*, *National Geographic Traveler*, *Washington Post Magazine*, *Harrowsmith*, and *Geo*. His images also appeared in the Voyageur Press books *This Old Tractor: A Treasury of Vintage Tractors and Family Farm Memories* and *The Complete Cow* and in numerous calendars. He lives in Paradise.